Y0-AEY-373

THE GUIDING HAND

AN OMF BOOK

© ALFRED BOSSHARDT AND EDWARD ENGLAND
c/o Edward England Books, Broadway House
The Broadway, Crowborough
East Sussex TN6 1BY
England

Published by Overseas Missionary Fellowship (IHQ) Ltd.,
2 Cluny Road, Singapore 1025,
Republic of Singapore

First published ... 19/3
New enlarged edition ... 1990

OMF BOOKS are distributed by
OMF, 404 South Church Street, Robesonia, Pa 19551, USA
OMF, Belmont, The Vine, Sevenoaks, Kent, TN13 3TZ, UK
OMF, P O Box 849, Epping, NSW 2121, Australia
OMF, 1058 Avenue Road, Toronto, Ontario M5N 2C6, Canada
OMF, P O Box 10159 Balmoral, Auckland, New Zealand
OMF, P O Box 41, Kenilworth 7745, South Africa
and other OMF offices.

ISBN 9971-972-98-0

Printed in Singapore
SW 5K/10/90

AUTHOR'S NOTE

The story of my captivity in China was told in *The Restraining Hand*, published in 1936. Reissuing the book had been considered, but instead, with Gwen and Edward England putting the words on paper for me, I have told something of God's goodness and mercy to me through a longer period – seventy-six years.

A.B.

In memory of my dear parents,
my sisters Ida, Freida and Lily
and my beloved Rose
all now with Christ

CONTENTS

INTRODUCTION

"IT'S A MIRACLE!" said 92-year-old Alfred Bosshardt, retired but still active CIM/OMFer. After fifty years of separation my arch-enemy General Xiao Ke has become my good friend."

Missionaries Bosshardt and Hayman were prisoners of General Xiao during the famous Chinese Communist "Long March". This book tells the story of how God protected and sustained His children through suffering as the "enemy" of a suffering army.

God's hand continued to guide. General Xiao, then head of the military academy in Beijing, renewed contact with Mr Bosshardt. After receiving a copy of *The Guiding Hand* the General asked his secretary to read it to him translating from English into Chinese. He was so impressed that he ordered the book to be published in Chinese. He wanted this new generation of Chinese leaders to understand a fuller portrayal of their history and the contribution of missionaries than the standard Party line provided.

God's hand will continue to guide as across China this book is read. As in the days of Cyrus so today, God's purposes are being fulfilled. We are grateful to General Xiao for his courageous action. We publish this edition of *The Guiding Hand* believing that you, by prayer, can have a vital role in God's on-going purpose of sharing the life and hope that come through Jesus Christ alone.

PROLOGUE

WE WERE TAKEN CAPTIVE in Communist hands – Rose and I, who had been man and wife for about three years. We loved each other, and our work as missionaries with the China Inland Mission, but it was our love for God which first united us. The Communists arrested seven of us, including two small children, but eventually kept only Arnolis Hayman and myself awaiting their demand for the payment of a fine of more than £70,000. We were part of their historic Long March. When the fine failed to reach our captor, General Hsiao Keh, a day was fixed for our execution.

Few doubted we would die.

Fresh in the minds of our friends were the recent deaths of two other CIM missionaries. In 1934 John and Betty Stam had also been accused of being imperialist spies. John had been one of a thousand students at the Moody Bible Institute, Chicago. Betty also was born in America but grew up in China where her parents were missionaries.

She met John at the Moody Bible Institute where they both attended the weekly missionary prayer meeting. They married in October, 1933 and their baby Helen Priscilla was born the following September. Soon after that the Communist soldiers came. John was twenty-seven and

Betty twenty-eight, somewhat younger than Rose and myself.

Their baby was miraculously saved from harm but in a clump of trees, on a small hillside outside the town, first John and then Betty, both on their knees, died. A friend who spoke for them was also killed.

Those were troubled days in China.

On the day of our public trial my wife was told that we had died. An eye witness of the execution of eight prisoners reported that we were among them.

But God had restrained the hand of our captors.

Why? – when John and Betty Stam died.

Who can pretend to know, but is it significant that while the Apostle James was beheaded Peter was released? With Peter there was time for the church to make supplication to God for him. And the church did.

Few knew of the arrest of John and Betty Stam: there was little time for special prayer on their behalf, the earnest prayer of God's people which might have stayed the sword, but the story of our prolonged captivity was in the world's newspapers and a multitude interceded.

Our magazine *China's Millions* urged: "We need to take the attitude of the Psalmist and say, 'I will cry unto God most high, unto God that performeth all things for me. He shall send from heaven and save me.' "

There were house prayer groups and bigger gatherings in Europe, America, Australia, New Zealand, South Africa, China, and other countries, on the eve of May 9, 1935.

Among those who prayed for us were the sorrowing families of John and Betty Stam.

It was believing prayer. A great cry. And God heard it. A journalist described in the *Daily Dispatch* the prayer meeting at my home church.

In a little mission hall in Manchester last night a hundred people bowed their heads in prayer. In far-away China two missionaries awaited death at the hands of bandits who have held them captive since last October. The thoughts of the congregation in Manchester spanned the 7,000 miles which separated them from the captives – one of whom they knew well – and in the midst of their supplications they wondered how they were faring. Perhaps they had been freed. Perhaps. . . . The meeting took place at the Union Hall Mission, in Vine Street, Hulme, from where Mr. R. A. Bosshardt, one of the missionaries, went on his perilous task with the China Inland Mission. Since he was captured, with a colleague, Mr. A. Hayman, the bandits have demanded a ransom of £70,000, and threatened, if it were not paid, to put them to death today. But of the anxiety in the hearts of the congregation in Mancheser last night there was little outward trace. They had come to show their belief that the fate of the missionaries was in the hands of a higher power than the bandits.

The superintendent, Mr. F. J. Thompson, smiling in spite of his fears, read to the congregation from the Acts of the Apostles an account of just such another gathering nearly 1900 years ago – a meeting of prayer for Peter, who had been imprisoned by Herod, which was eventually terminated by the appearing of Peter himself, freed by the angel of the Lord. "Whilst our love for dear brother Alfred Bosshardt is great," said the Superintendent, "we have got a greater love than that. Our first love, and he would have it so, is our love for the Lord. Men of the world will do heroic things for any they love. Distance prevents us from doing anything like that, and perhaps the most heroic thing we are going to tell God – what is very hard for our hearts to tell Him – is that whatever is, is best. I believe that great things are going to be done in China tonight. I believe that great things are going to be done here. Would it not be wonderful if out of the intensity of this meeting someone stepped out and said, 'I am going to tell China, not to tell the brigands what we think about them, but to tell them that Jesus died for them'?" Referring to the bandits* in another prayer, Mr. Thompson quoted Jesus's words: "Father, forgive them, for they know not what they do." Then, one after the other, men and women in the congregation added their earnest prayers, while the rest fervently murmured assent.

A *Daily Dispatch* reporter went from the meeting to the home of Mr. Bosshardt's parents in King's Road, Chorlton-cum-Hardy. They had been expected at the Mission Hall, but had not arrived, though their daughter and her husband were present. Mrs. Bosshardt said sadly: "I should like to have been there, but I could not face it." Her face lit up when she was told the meeting had been an excellent one. "We can only wait and pray," she said.

---

*This report speaks of bandits. They were in fact the convinced Communists who now rule China. What they did was legitimate in their eyes; imperialist spies were executed; a fine was an amelioration.

1

RAVENS IN CHINA

JUST OCCASIONALLY YOU FIND yourself at a decisive point in life, at a day on which years to come seem to hinge. Such an event occurred in my life when I was a boy of ten. A missionary came home from China to Moss Side Baptist church in Manchester. His ringing challenge was for adults, but I shared the hush of the listening congregation.

Charles Fairclough was a single man, on furlough after ten years, a colourful, energetic figure, who spoke Chinese with the barest trace of a Lancashire accent. He was to return to China on October 9, 1907. No one knew better than he that he was an unimportant person, but every word communicated that he believed he was doing the most privileged job in the world. A witness. A mouthpiece to men.

From that day I was set for China. It's where I wanted to be.

Mr. Fairclough told how his own society, the China Inland Mission, and others had pioneered the inland provinces, and of the millions still unreached. Most of the missionaries from our church, fourteen in all, were with the zealous Baptist Missionary Society, so he explained about the CIM. When it started there were only fifteen

Protestant mission stations in China, with about 2,000 converts. Now the Mission alone had 205 central stations and 632 out-stations, with more than 14,000 converts. On January 1, 1906 it had 849 missionaries, assisted by 1,282 Chinese helpers. It had 476 organised churches, 188 day and boarding schools, seven hospitals, 37 dispensaries, and 101 opium refuges. During 1906 there were 3,500 baptisms.

The danger and adventure of a missionary's life conquered my imagination.

Mr. Fairclough had little formal education, yet he had learned the Chinese language and much that was never taught in a university. He believed that his God was more than adequate for any of his inadequacies. He had been commended to work in China by a group of evangelical ministers from various denominations, among them, Dr. F. B. Meyer and Dr. Campbell Morgan.

The Chinese Empire became in our minds like a new suburb of Manchester, and Charles Fairclough sought it for God. Following the rule of his society, he made no appeal for money – not a hint of it – but we gave even when we hardly had the tram fare home. If there had been a tramcar to China we would have jumped aboard, our God providing the fare. I gained the vivid impression, which has never deserted me, that God is sometimes limited by a bank balance, but never by the lack of it.

Dr. Meyer came to Moss Side for his valedictory service and gave the address. About one thousand crowded in. There was a restrained excitement and a lump in my throat. I might not see my new friend in Manchester again. In one year fifty-eight CIM missionaries and twenty-two children had died. When one died another replaced him. Could I be one?

Drink, it was said, was the quickest way out of

Manchester, and the sad poverty in some mean streets made a quick exit desirable, but I had no complaints about the city. For my Swiss parents it had seemed brighter since their conversion, as our church under Rev. Arnold Streuli's ministry was experiencing revival. There were adult baptisms twice a month as the congregation swelled from 200 to more than 800.

There was plenty of sooty rain and damp fog, poverty showing in poor footwear and frayed cuffs, and the threat of unemployment, but a light flooded our Christian life, making dark areas less gloomy. Too many depended on the textile industry in this cotton metropolis, but as so often the treasure of heaven was found by some of the very poorest.

When I was sixteen we went to the Swanwick Conference Centre for an interchurch missionary gathering. On my return, with a new authority, I was asked to report on the China situation at meetings of young people.

This same year Mao Tse-tung, who was to become one of the most powerful political leaders of the twentieth century, was entering the Fourth Provincial Normal School of Changsha, which was to be a training ground for his apprenticeship as a political worker. Revolutionary intentions were born.

In a more ordered world we collected for missions. The Juvenile Missionary Auxiliary issued cards to solicit funds, each card having a space for twelve names. Weekly sums of a halfpenny and a penny were called for. I had three full cards, and usually collected more than anyone else, until one day I read a book *Faith and Facts* by Marshall Broomhall, which caused an upheaval in my thinking.

I saw what the faith principle of the CIM meant. I grasped what was meant by a faith mission which did not ask men for money. CIM looked to God for financial support. It had no collecting tins or cards, its founder no doubt being influenced by his friend George Muller of Bristol who looked to God alone for the needs of his many orphan children. This policy had its critics, but Hudson Taylor believed that God had called him and all who joined his Mission to walk this path of faith.

> We can afford to have as little as the Lord chooses to give, but we cannot afford to have unconsecrated money. Far better have no money at all, even to buy food with; for there are plenty of ravens in China, and the Lord could send them again with bread and flesh. . . . Our Father is a very experienced one. He knew very well that his children wake up with a good appetite every morning, and he always provides breakfast for them, and does not send them supperless to bed.

Plenty of ravens in China. . . . The lack of money was a slow-down signal, a red warning light, in Christian mission. Could one entirely trust God and his ravens? Dare I tread this way.

I turned my energy from collecting to encouraging prayer for God's pioneers, leaving the Holy Spirit to prompt informed Christians of their responsibilities. Some pennies were lost. They had been given reluctantly, and with no weekly reminder the donors were happy to forget, but the total missionary giving went up.

Five of us covenanted to contribute the full support of a Korean theological student in the Oriental Missionary Society at Seoul. We met to consider reports of his progress and to pray for him.

A monthly Saturday evening meeting in our home developed into a weekly missionary prayer group, supported by twenty to thirty from various churches. As we prayed for those overseas we were quickened about people in our neighbourhood, on fine evenings holding open-air services, often opposite the cinema queue.

"Not only our money, Lord . . ." we prayed.

About twelve of our members gave up their jobs for full-time Christian service.

When our pastor was replaced by a man with a different theological outlook, a few of us left to join Union Hall Mission Church, an off-shoot of Dr. Alexander McClaren's famous Union Chapel. The superintendent was Francis Thompson.

My father came from the Canton of Zurich, following his elder brother to Manchester, where he worked first in engineering and later with his brother who became a patent agent. In this new employment my father met a young Swiss woman from St. Gallen teaching embroidery by machine. They were engaged, married in Switzerland, and returned to establish their home in Manchester.

I was apprenticed as an engineer. Overtime during the First World War meant missing many evening classes, but later I made up for lost study attending the Manchester Technical College on Mondays.

In my teens I read the two-volume life of J. Hudson Taylor: *The Growth of a Soul* and *The Growth of a Work of God* by Dr. and Mrs. Howard Taylor. Again I saw what God can do with a man wholly surrendered. God's dealing with Hudson Taylor came as a revelation, and his burden for a million Chinese a month dying without the Gospel. The burden was burned into his very soul. For two or three months the conflict was intense. He scarcely slept night or day more than an hour at a time, and feared he would lose his reason.

Some weeks later, on Sunday, June 25, 1865, on a quiet

Sunday morning, too burdened to go to church, while walking on the sands in Brighton he prayed for twenty-four evangelists. He wanted two each for the twelve unoccupied provinces of inland China. Two days later he opened an account for the China Inland Mission and paid in £10. The CIM was born.

He believed in plain living and high thinking, I read, in Chinese dress, Chinese food and Chinese ways. New arrivals in Shanghai recorded how Mr. Taylor took them to a native cook shop for a meal, where four narrow forms were placed around a table. The cooking was done in the front part of the shop.

> Our table had once been new, and probably had once been clean, but it must have been many years before we were born. However, what it lacked in purity it made up in polish. . . . A pair of chopsticks was brought and placed before each of us, after having been carefully wiped on the shady cloth which dangled over the shoulder of the attendant.

A year after my apprenticeship ended at twenty-two, I applied to the CIM to be a candidate for China. There was no question of my desire but I was hesitant of my natural ability and of my spiritual maturity, but the conviction grew that I should apply. I was under no illusion about the life of a missionary in China.

I had little to give except my youth. I had read of the Cambridge Seven and of the university men who had offered themselves after Mr. Taylor's visit to America. The finest men and women were required for God's work. I was not in that category. My talents were commonplace. Was there a place for ordinary people as missionaries?

The letter with the London postmark duly arrived, and

I was invited to attend the CIM conference at Swanwick in Derbyshire where the Council would meet, which would save the expense of a visit to London. It was where I had attended the interchurch missionary get-together.

"May the Council make the right decision," I prayed.

Swanwick is surrounded by nature's lovely places, almost in the heart of England, and among the crags and dells, the streams and rocky wildness, it was easy to pray and praise, but I was not entirely at ease.

As I faced the Council, good men, conscious of their heavy responsibility, I felt very immature. They were courteous but searching in their questions, guardians of the Mission and the faith. They invited me to spend three months at the training home in London, but could give no definite indication whether or not I would be accepted.

"It will mean giving up your job," they warned gravely. "After three months we may suggest you return home."

They did not need to spell out the implications.

There was unemployment throughout Britain with long queues of dispirited ex-servicemen at labour exchanges. I was twenty-three and this was my first step of faith.

God had his ravens.

Mr. Taylor had wanted all candidates to spend such a period in London for personal acquaintance. He believed that the only ones who would be happy with the Mission were those "who have this world under their feet," who "count all things but dross and dung for the excellency of the knowledge of Jesus Christ our Lord".

Did anyone completely measure up to this?

The Mission had attracted men and women with exceptional qualifications but "while thankful for any educational advantages that candidates may have enjoyed," he wrote, "we attach far greater importance to spiritual qualifications. We desire men who believe that there is a

God and that he is both intelligent and faithful, and who therefore trust him; who believe that he is the rewarder of those who diligently seek him, and are therefore men of prayer. We desire men who believe the Bible to be the word of God, and who accepting the declaration, 'All power is given unto me,' are prepared to carry out to the best of their ability the command, 'Go . . . teach all nations,' relying on him who possesses 'all power' and has promised to be with his messengers 'always'."

There was a small, jovial group to send me off from the Manchester station. My cycle had gone in advance by rail and I collected it at St. Pancras station. I had been told the number 73 London bus went to the CIM headquarters, so I wheeled my bicycle from the station into the heavy traffic and prepared to follow it. At one bus stop I recognised a missionary. He shook hands with me when he got off, showed me my destination, and later escorted me round the Mission building.

"Over the doorway leading to the prayer hall and facing the green," I wrote home, "are the words cut in stone *Have faith in God.*"

"It means you, Alfred," I told myself, "and everyone who enters."

Hudson Taylor had written in the latter part of his life: "God is willing to give us all we need, as we need it. He does not equip for life-service all *at once.* . . And whatever the sufficiency of Christ is for *us,* there is the same sufficiency in him for all our converts."

Our talk, our prayers, our dreams, were of China, of coolies, beggars, merchants and magistrates. I went with two other students to London's Chinatown. Our declared intention was to buy Chinese pens, but we included a Chinese meal in a dirty restaurant. We were the only Europeans and we coped awkwardly with our chopsticks.

In three months of communal living, eating, praying, studying together, those responsible began to get some insight into our abilities and character. They saw the grey as well as the golden areas. Whatever my failings the Council decided that I should remain for the full two years Biblical and practical training.

Mondays were set apart for medical training at the Old Ford Medical Mission, a cycle ride away across London. Our tutor, Dr. Tom Bragg, had been in China and knew that in the interior we would find few hospitals or nurses, and would be faced with frightening situations. Most of the peasants died without seeing a qualified practitioner. There were days when he had terrible misgivings about us, as we tied ourselves in knots with bandages, and confidently prescribed the wrong remedies.

"Admirable," he would say on the rare occasions when he could. We would never make doctors, but unless we had confidence we would never make anything. Our hours with him were among the most important of our training, going far beyond normal first aid. We assisted in compounding ointments, dispensing medicine and reading prescriptions. After diagnosis he would instruct us in the steps to be taken. In the consulting rooms we caught glimpses of the courage of patients and the strains of the doctor.

Dr. Bragg withheld nothing, knowing from his experience, what we would face in China. His lectures introduced us to new words and new worlds.

How quickly the months went, how often in future years we would look back to them and to the friendships made. The Home Director, Dr. Stuart Holden, was a man of God, and we treasured our occasional meetings.

The day came when we made our decisive appearance before the Council to be told whether we would sail. At this juncture there was love but no place for sentiment as they sought to know the will of God.

I cannot recall all they asked me, but I do remember being questioned as to whether I had any personal experience of God's provision of material needs? They placed importance on that. I thought hard.

"There's one thing," I said.

Before I left Manchester I had saved the fare for my passage to China, but had expected I would need to use it for expenses over the two years of training for fares, clothes, books. The fare was still intact. God had met every need without touching it. And to me it seemed a miracle.

When I heard the Council's decision I glowed with happiness. They shared my conviction that God had called me, with no academic qualifications, for China. There would be years of language study ahead, and because I had the hands of an apprentice rather than the mind of a student that would not be easy.

About 2,000 supporters crowded into Kingsway Hall, London, on September 12, 1922, to say farewell to the eleven new recruits. The chair was taken by Lt. Col. J. Winn who offered suggestions as to how interest in China and the missionaries might be maintained. His own habit was to spend half an hour each day in prayer for China and the CIM. He prayed with a map before him, and found it one of the fascinations of his life to underline with red ink every new place on that map which was opened as a mission station.

The preacher was Pastor D. M. Panton who spoke of Elisha's deliverance from the army of Benhahad, King of Syria. He described two men, helpless, unarmed, caught in a cordon of steel, so that one of them cried to the other: "Alas, master, what shall we do?" It is in a situation like that, he reminded us, that the prophet says, "Lord, open the young man's eyes, that he may see. And, lo, the mountain was white with the hosts of God."

He closed his address with recalling Raphael, the great painter, commissioned to paint a portrait of the Lord Jesus. He obtained a New Testament and day after day was seen, brush in hand, with it open before him, every feature riveted and every thought absorbed; until suddenly one day he slipped upon his knees and cried, "My Lord and my God! " The picture was never painted, but God had stamped an image on Raphael's soul that would never be obliterated.

Afterwards I was reunited with my mother who had come from Manchester for the service. She knew my imperfections. I knew that my departure was going to be costly for her. A current of understanding and love passed between us. She was praying, *Lord help me to give him to you fully.*

2

NEW WORLD

VERY TRUE AND REAL in her love, mother remained at CIM headquarters in London for a few days helping me to pack. My admiration and affection for her deepened as she endeavoured to conceal the cost of parting. I wrote to the rest of the family telling how I had been thinking and picturing them.

> The disturbing of deep roots, however gently done is very painful and one feels the wrench now, though another is to come when I say goodbye to mother. It is such a comfort to have her here. How richly God is comforting me. Yesterday as I prayed and thanked the Lord for the love of an earthly father, I felt the arms of my Heavenly Father around me. . . Mother bought me a beautiful Bible. I took her to the Scripture Gift Mission and got a considerable reduction. She will inscribe it for me.

On September 28 she accompanied me to the London docks to see the *Kitana Maru,* the Japanese boat on which I would sail. A polite, bowing Japanese officer showed us all we wanted to see, including the cabin. There would be seven passengers, second class, to Marseilles,

where more would come aboard. Mother was a little subdued as we returned to Newington Green.

"On Friday," she said gently, "I'll say goodbye to you
at the station."

Something told me that would be best. The leaves were
turning brown and golden, an early sign of autumn, as we
reached Newington Green, an address known to Christians
in five continents.

"But now you'll be able to think of me on the boat."

We read of missionaries, rarely of their mothers, but
so much is owed to their prayers and sacrifice, to their
love and shining belief.

A railway carriage full of friends came to the docks,
playful, excited, almost envious, as they came on board.
One expressed disappointment, but the accommodation
was really adequate. The party left to catch their train –
we did not sail until dawn – and I was left alone. I examined the beautiful copy of *Great Souls at Prayer* which
my former pastor, Mr. Streuli, had given me. As the boat
prepared to weigh anchor I wrote to mother.

I could not trust myself to speak. Perhaps my very
silence spoke louder than words. My own dear mother,
may God richly bless you. Thank you very much for
coming up, for it has been a real comfort to have you
but I am afraid it was no treat for you. . . Glory to
God who loved us and spared not his only Son for us.
We know more what this means now, don't we,
mother?

Feeling tired I went to bed early, but did not sleep
well – a strange bed, noisy crew, weird deck sounds, and
my mixed feelings, accounted for this. About 6.30 a.m.,
peering out of the porthole, I saw we were moving, so

slowly that the movement was not perceptible inside the cabin. It was a glorious morning, clear and crisp, and full of promise; we were towed slowly from one dock to another and then into the river. I breathed in with my mind the smell of the open water and life on deck.

In one dock men were standing within reach. I hastily scribbled my envelope, popped the letter inside which I had intended posting home from France, and threw it over the side, with a tip, for a docker to post. Boat drill followed. At the sounding of the alarm bell we put on our life-jackets and took our stations.

Two other CIM recruits, Reginald Bazire and Gordon Welch, joined us at Marseilles. As the three of us walked the shadowy streets that Saturday night, we met a small band of Salvationists out pubbing, selling the French edition of the *War Cry*. We crossed to buy a copy. As one of the officers who had trained in London knew English we prayed together by a street lamp, parting with repeated hallelujahs.

On reaching Singapore a Chinese student who had been studying in Newcastle invited Gordon Welch and myself to his home and country club.

A feast was given by the student, attended by six Chinese. We each had a pair of chopsticks, bowl, a porcelain spoon and a tiny saucer of sauce. In the centre of the table was the dish of food from which we helped ourselves, taking pieces of pork, chicken, fish, prawns, bird's nest, seaweed and pastry. We lost count of the number of courses.

The student who had wealthy parents had started a youth club before going to England, and he invited me to address it. This was my first Chinese gathering.

I tried to speak to a coolie.

"I no savvy you, you no savvy me," he said when we failed to communicate.

When we reached Hong Kong on November 12 among the first sights was a Chinese funeral. I wrote home:

It was a very long procession, with crude images of gods surrounded by artificial flowers and coloured paper. There were food offerings – whole roast pig and goat and vegetables – all carried under canopies, while little boys had banners and lanterns, followed by friends in rickshaws. The chief mourners wore unbleached white cloth with hoods and gowns. A Chinese band formed part of the procession, and priests in saffron gowns chanted. The eldest son was assisted on either side as he walked with bowed head. The huge coffin, carried by coolies, came last. It was quite an experience to see all this before reaching my destination. Back on board I lay on deck feeling refreshed. After dark the harbour became like fairyland.

Two or three days later we were in Shanghai. While coolies looked after our baggage we went by rickshaw through the busy streets, with peddlars selling food from the roadside, and signs of abundance and frightening poverty. Suddenly we turned off and found ourselves in the beautiful compound of the CIM where everything spoke of peace and love. What a contrast – the turmoil outside and the quiet within the gates.

We spent five days there.

Shanghai is a great metropolis, sitting on the river Huang Pu, fifteen miles from the estuary of the mighty Yangtse Kiang. It is centrally situated as a port on the China coast, and is the point of departure for most interior travel. We repacked our possessions for the journey inland.

To a meeting of about fifty, including older missionaries bearing the marks of hardship and persecution, we told of God's call. They knew what lay ahead and where we would find our resources. Their faith and their patience in suffering had given them a rich tranquillity, an inner vitality which pierced the spirits of untried, raw beginners.

When we had finished, D. E. Hoste, the Director who had succeeded Hudson Taylor, spoke. He was one of the Cambridge Seven, who had been a young officer in the Royal Artillery before offering himself for China. After being superintendent of South Shansi, he became acting Director until 1902 when Hudson Taylor resigned to give him the full direction of the Mission.

This legendary figure carried enormous responsibility, but it was arranged that we took it in turns to sit next to him at meals. We listened to him with awe. He advised me about fitness in China, what to accept and what to avoid. He warned against allowing barriers between myself and the Chinese, and spoke of the need to be crucified daily, allowing one's rights to be trampled on, remembering that the servant is not greater than his Lord.

In Shanghai we purchased equipment for travel in China: bedding, a large oil sheet, a fibre mat, a basket for odds and ends, a Chinese-English dictionary, primers, a large character New Testament and books for language study. We visited a Chinese home, dispensary, girls' school and club for students, and developed our taste for Chinese food.

Since Marseilles, five weeks earlier, I had had no news of my family.

There were no home letters waiting me on arrival, but don't think I am complaining – they will be all the sweeter when they arrive. This letter must bring you my Christmas greetings. It will be the first time we have not been a complete family for the occasion. Yet, but for the first Christmas, I would not be here.

On November 19 we left Shanghai for the language school at Chinkiang, where Hudson Taylor and his wife had once made their home. The staff saw us off as we left the compound in rickshaws for the train. My coolie tried to squeeze between two wheel-barrows heavily laden with tiles, succeeding in knocking them over. Without a look behind him he ran on, but the indignant barrowmen with much abuse caught him up, and a crowd gathered. There was almost a fight but a senior missionary put things right, saving an unpleasant scene.

In Chinkiang we were met by Samuel Glanville. We carried our lighter luggage from the train to the mission house, the rest following by barrow. For the fifteen-minute walk we were pestered by coolies and wizened beggars.

At the house I found, to my delight, that Mrs. Glanville had spent two years in Manchester training at Star Hall, nearly twenty years before.

As well as the three of us from Britain there were two new workers from Sweden, two from Australia, and Mr. and Mrs. Herbert Griffin with their little boy from America. Others were to come. We each had a room to ourselves, combining bedroom and study. With the zeal of those at the start of a race we began our lessons on Saturday, the day after our arrival.

Our teacher was Mr. Lui. Before we met him we were instructed how to enter his presence and shown how to bow. Those who wore spectacles raised them as a token of respect. Mr. Lui started by teaching us Chinese sounds and tones, and how thankful we were then for the phonetic classes in London, especially as he knew no English.

He gave us Chinese names. Mine was Boh-Sha-Teo. The first character, according to the dictionary meant thin; slight, poor, mean, ungenerous, stingy, contemptuous, careless. However, the other two characters modified this and the whole read something like – although thin and small he has understanding and discernment. My name was later changed in Kweichow to Boh Fu-li, meaning unselfish.

There was six hours' study daily, with lights out at 10 p.m. and the rising bell at 6 a.m. Each day we spent a period alone with our teacher, had two group lessons with him and attended a grammar lesson given by Mr. Glanville. Twice a week we had lessons on how to write with a Chinese pen.

"I have found that there are three stages," Hudson Taylor said with regard to some matter. "First, it is impossible, then it is difficult, then it is done."

Had the letters from home, which I expected to be waiting for me on arrival in China, gone astray or been stolen? Surely, mother would have written. Perhaps something was wrong.

It was only ten days – it seemed ages – after stepping on to Chinese soil that the first letters came. I was about to enter class, but there was no opportunity to read them so all morning they burned in my pocket. Courtesy demanded that I gave the teacher full attention.

In the privacy of my room, I read the mail, visualising those I would not see for seven years. Physically I had arrived in China, but my heart was making the journey more slowly!

"The cross does not get comfortable," Hudson Taylor warned.

Next door to the language school was a Buddhist convent where the gong went incessantly, but it was one of the less strange noises which penetrated our classrooms and bedrooms. Vendors called or clacked bamboos, and small boys leading the blind rang their bell every few seconds as they progressed along the road. Coolies accompanied their rhythmic swing with heh ho, heh ho, and every barrowman called for a clearway.

Our ears had to get accustomed to Chinese singing. On our first Sunday in chapel we tried not to be appalled. Mr. Glanville preached in Chinese and the text was written out beforehand on the blackboard so all could repeat it. There were forty present, the women sitting separately from the men.

Pray for me especially as I acclimatise (I wrote home). I have been well so far. Study is a real grind – my head aches sometimes. I don't want to get out of this habit of sending a weekly letter. This week has been busier as it has been my turn to attend Chinese prayers. First we sing a hymn in Chinese. The five servants, the gateman, the two teachers, Mr. and Mrs. Glanville, and four students attend each day. Each one reads a verse of Scripture. During the weekend we had Mr. and Mrs. Saunders staying with us from Yangchow. He is blind and she just about stone deaf, both afflictions caused by the suffering during the Boxer troubles. Mr. Saunders preached at the Sunday service and the Chinese listened intently. I get very tired and have overslept two or three times, so I will have to watch myself.

The founder of the Mission, I knew, had been an early riser. Before dawn, before the Chinese stirred, he was sitting up praying and reading with the light of two candles.

My first Christmas away from home! We walked for an hour to find a tree, and bought brightly coloured decorations. At breakfast we came down to find cards on our plates from the Glanvilles and the Hostes. Mr. Hoste's bore the text: "Fear not, for I am with thee, I will strengthen, I will help, I will uphold." After the meal Mr. Glanville gave us a promise from the book of Ruth: "Thou hast left thy father and mother and the land of thy nativity and art come unto a people thou knewest not heretofore. The Lord recompense thy work and a full reward be given thee of the Lord God of Israel, under whose wings thou art come to trust."

"God has dealt most tenderly with me," I wrote, "giving me the desires of my heart and weaning me from things I have held dear."

The cold weather came with the New Year and I woke to find a thick layer of ice in the water jug in my room, but more important I had now learned the Lord's prayer in Chinese! Not that this achievement proved of much consequence as I walked along the main street of Chinkiang, three miles long.

Every step gave cause for wonder. I had imagined that the main street of a town of 300,000 inhabitants would be a fine affair, but this was only the width of the average pavement at home, with enough room for two wheel-barrows to pass. Beggars, mostly professional, abounded. One poor man without feet propelled himself along with his hands. To excite pity he had shaved his head and placed lighted incense sticks in a large hole in the skull, probably the result of a self-inflicted wound.

The narrow street was lined on either side with shops and stalls, opening directly on to the street. Nothing was done in private. Men had their heads shaved by the barber on the street. Likewise the dentist had his stall, with a long string of teeth that he had extracted, which were his recommendation. The children of the beggars trained to cry, were a sad sight, but even more numerous than the children were the dogs, seeming to belong to no one, seeking food. Then there were the fowls and pigs. And always the burden-bearers. The rich and middle class were drawn about in rickshaws. I marvelled at how much the coolies would carry for a pittance. If an article was too heavy for one man, two would take it, and for a very heavy load as many as forty might be called into service.

Among all the babble it was refreshing to stop at a small street chapel, and see it full of people, quietly seated, listening to an evangelist. As a foreigner I was a curiosity. If I stopped to make a purchase there was soon a group of spectators.

In the spring Mr. Hoste came to designate us to various parts of China. We all had areas which we favoured but we would be told where the Mission wanted us to go. On the Saturday before my interview I went for a long walk. As I strode along, I had the conviction that Mr. Hoste would know God's place for me.

When I went in to see him, after the preliminaries, he said, "Let us have some prayer together." He had a map of China on the table. When he finished praying he pointed to Tsunyi, the second largest town in Kweichow, where there was a long-established church.

From that moment it was my objective. I believed that God had chosen it as my destination. Mr. and Mrs. Oleson, senior missionaries, had temporarily left the station to take their children to school. An encounter with robbers on the journey had badly frightened Mrs. Oleson but now she was prepared to go back, and I would accompany them.

The Director looked at me as he spoke and I believe he saw the glad acceptance in my eyes.

He was a lonely man, isolated by his nature rather than his position. I was once privileged to join him in his prayer-time. Having someone in the room was a help to his concentration as for two hours he paced up and down, praying aloud, mentioning the names of all CIM missionaries and their children. Age had not robbed him of his memory or concern.

Years later, he was to invite my wife and me to join him and Mrs. Hoste – a semi-invalid – for tea in their bedroom.

The previous Christmas when we were at Kiang Wan Bible School we had sent them a small portion of butter. It was marked "home-made" and was from the rich milk we were getting. When we went into their room we saw the butter in the soapdish.

"Thank you for your gift," Mrs. Hoste beamed, having put it in the washstand prior to our arrival.

"But it's not soap," we stammered.

The departure to Tsunyi was delayed. Because of his specialist knowledge Mr. Oleson had to oversee the building of the war memorial hall at our Chefoo schools, and I was sent to Chungking for nine months to continue language studies. I had been there a few weeks when two telegrams arrived from Manchester.

One informed me of the serious illness of my sister, Freida. The other of her death, a few days before her thirtieth birthday. I shut my eyes and saw her image.

I long at this time to be able to throw my arms around you and comfort your sore hearts. I only have the bare facts in three words. The tears will come. How awfully sudden and yet I believe the Lord has been preparing our hearts. The Lord is comforting me although I am far from everyone who knew her. I do weep with you. I know my heart will go out in a new way to the many bereaved in this land.

Later that month I received the last letter my sister wrote to me, posted two months earlier.

Correspondence had assumed a new importance in my life.

3

THE INTERIOR

MY LETTERS HOME WERE not penned thoughtlessly, but they caused anxiety. I was not impulsive in what I wrote, never wishing to create a state of alarm, but if I did not give the facts intelligent prayer was less likely. What does a missionary in a troubled situation share with his family? I was not the first to ask the question. Re-reading the letters which I wrote in early years, preserved by mother, I can better understand her concern, but she always insisted she wanted me to tell everything, otherwise she would worry, about what I was withholding!

If soldiers were not fighting in the vicinity, bandits were plundering. A journey of two or three days in the interior meant trouble. Communications were difficult, proper roads non-existent for thousands of miles. There were no hospitals or doctors within easy reach. Foreigners excited curiosity.

God's loving care was ever with us, but he did not necessarily save us from physical harm or even death.

For those in China fear was often relieved by action, and the strain was not necessarily prolonged, but at home they lived with uncertainty, especially if a letter was a cliff-hanger.

The gap between the weekly letters must have been an eternity.

I never exaggerated. To avoid distress I should probably have gone further in the other direction. Healthy young men take kindly to a little adventure spiced with danger but love demands that it is modestly recounted.

In July 1923 Chungking was besieged for a week. We were in the hills for the summer but one missionary, with cook and coolie, who had gone for provisions, was trapped in the city for days while it was bombarded. The general-in-command was known as the butcher. Missionaries who attended his feast had fainted when prisoners were ill-treated before being killed.

In August there was fighting in the city. A missionary had a marvellous escape when a bullet skimmed past his head, and the general apologised to the foreign community for their disturbed nights. Soon he and his troops left the city leaving behind the dead and wounded.

A week later, spending a night in the city, I was awakened by firing from the other side of the river – another siege had started.

We are still in it. As staying awake would not help matters, I lay down again and slept like a top. The next day many soldiers were killed or drowned trying to cross the river. The city gates were shut and no water was allowed into the city. Rice was practically unobtainable. The bigger shops were barricaded against looting. There were many executions. We saw one sad procession with two condemned men escorted by a company of soldiers. The execution ground was crowded with spectators. The condemned men were in rags, their hands bound, with a placard on them telling their crime.
One lot seems as bad as another. I slept so well last night that there is no need for you to be anxious.

I moved out of the city to stay with Mr. and Mrs. Curtis in Kiangtsin, higher up the Yangtse. They had a delightful Chinese home. Opposite my room was the school where from dawn the children shouted their lessons. I visited tea shops and homes with literature, inviting people to our Sunday service. Life here was more peaceful although homes were being looted and we saw the bodies of four soldiers killed in the street.

I received permission to visit the prison, unbelievably overcrowded and terribly filthy, with a stench that hit the nostrils. Wide-opened eyes were dulled from hunger. I gave out leaflets and tried to make myself understood. At least, my visit was a diversion.

An instruction was given that ten thousand meals of boiled rice had to be prepared for the tired, hungry soldiers who would pass through Kiangtsin. Women, fearing their arrival, asked if they could sleep on our premises.

Mr. and Mrs. Curtis had been missionaries in Kiangtsin for seventeen years and were accepted by the Chinese as their own. In the street passers-by spoke to them as father and mother. On Sundays there were about fifty adults in chapel plus eighty school girls and boys. Between language studies I accompanied Mr. Curtis to the market selling up to five hundred Gospels in a day. We had to watch for savage dogs. I had two nasty experiences. One tore my clothes and bit my leg.

Food was so scarce in Chungking that I remained in Kiangtsin until November when I returned to link up with Mr. and Mrs. Oleson and Miss Brock (later Mrs. Will Windsor) for the long journey to Tsunyi.

We set out on December 4 with coolies, making up a party of seventeen, first crossing the Yangtse. We took a last look at Chungking and the river that stretched to Shanghai, then pressed towards the inn where we would spend the night. Our luggage had been packed into 100 lb. loads for carrying.

The journey was to be in ten stages over ten days. The women had sedan chairs and the men walked in straw sandals. Mrs. Oleson, because of her previous experience with bandits, was both very frightened and very courageous. It was a natural, healthy fear, but as she set her face westwards I learned what courage was.

After three days we reached an out-station where there were rumours of bandits ahead.

We were so well on the way to Tsunyi that I could hardly bear the thought of a further postponement. I had waited months. I was sickened by the stories, weary of travelling without arriving.

"God, take us through," I breathed impatiently.

The Olesons told God in their prayers we would go forward unless he prevented us. The next morning, after troubled sleep, an official confronted us.

"It's impossible," he said. "You must return to Chungking."

Mr. Oleson refused, negotiating for us to travel with a commercial caravan with an escort of two hundred soldiers.

My spirits rose. But not for long. Our way was soon blocked by heavy firing. The coolies dropped their loads and ran for shelter, while we took refuge in a temple. As we huddled listening to the guns, we reluctantly accepted that God was allowing us to be prevented and turned back. There was no alternative.

It has been a great disappointment to return. It was a much more dangerous affair than when we came. We passed unharmed through a large band of robbers. It seemed touch and go. But the Lord covered us.

In Chungking the Olesons had to make a big decision. Should Mrs. Oleson and Miss Brock be left, while Mr. Oleson and I made a further attempt to reach Tsunyi? The Christians there were waiting for us. Mrs. Oleson was distressed at the prospect of prolonged separation, at the dangers of the journey, but she would not hold back her husband. In a few weeks, or months, she and Miss Brock might make the journey with a suitable escort.

"Go," she said bravely. "And God be with you."

She took me on one side and told me about life in Tsunyi, about the food, the opportunities and the setbacks. We prayed together and said our goodbyes.

Whichever way we go there will be danger. My New Year text is: "Say not, I am a child: for thou shalt go to all I send thee and whatsoever I command thee thou shalt speak." I am twenty-seven today. Truly I am getting an old man.

At first we had an escort of thirty soldiers on our detour route. We spent three days in Chinkiang and found that Mr. Lan, who had been with us on the last trip, had been shot as a spy. We had letters of introduction to an ex-brigand chief who held the road to the Kweichow border and they proved effective. We walked thirty miles in one day over bad roads, climbing weary hills. With a full load for our coolies it was quite exacting but the soldiers used the butt end of their rifles to urge them on, and we seemed helpless to prevent it.

Village after village had been plundered. Mr. Oleson and I mused on Psalms, learning some by heart. "I will both lay me down in peace to sleep, for thou only makest me to dwell in safety," we repeated, thinking of Christians over the centuries who in danger had found strength in these words.

One night saw us, a group of twelve men, sitting around a fire on low benches. The fire was an anthracite heap in the middle of a room, hot and smokeless. The room was bare, but how wonderful just to sit and rest. A boy held a candle to give us light. We discussed the possibilities for the next day and were advised to join a caravan going through to Tsunyi, our destination. The caravan consisted of salt carriers, a company of Yunnan soldiers without rifles stranded in Szechwan, and a few armed soldiers. It seemed a perfect idea.

We journeyed through rough country, along one cliff with a sheer drop of 1,000 feet. The scenery was magnificent, worth the fatigue, although our feet were blistered and our bodies wet with exertion.

If I wavered I was encouraged by the immenseness of Mr. Oleson's faith.

We walked twenty-five miles that day, fixing our bedding in one of the farmhouses where the officers claimed rooms. Not knowing who were to be feared or trusted some peasants had fled at our arrival.

The following day I became separated from the main body, without food, bedding or friends. We had just crossed the border into Kweichow province. My feet were bleeding. The few soldiers with me lit a big coal fire and we gathered round. The others would catch us up the next day. All must pass that way. But Mr. Oleson was frantically searching, and caught me up after walking round a couple of hours in the dark. Fear for me had besieged his imagination, and I had no wish to conceal my own delight at seeing him.

Kweichow as originally written meant the Land of Demons. It was 66,000 square miles, with a population of nearly seventeen million who lived in dread of demons. Now it is written the Worthy Region. Products include rice, wheat, maize, tung oil, mercury and silk. Among the exports was opium. The province had no roads for wheeled traffic. The roads were of rough stones, with flights of steps when there was a gradient. Wheels could not be used. Everything had to be carried. The first missionaries had gone there in 1887.

In a farmhouse where the owners had never before seen foreigners, as there was no available bed, we put two square tables together and put our bedding on them. We had an oil lamp with a pith wick for lighting, and little else for comfort, but I was so full of joy that God had at last brought me to this province.

"The tenth anniversary of my baptism," I told Mr. Oleson, no longer so tired, immeasurably happy, and on the doorstep of Tsunyi. I wrote there and then to my pastor, Mr. Streuli, to share with him my joy.

Our three-week detour ended in Tsunyi in February. Normally, by the direct route, the journey would have taken ten days. My feet were so bad it was painful to put them down, but my heart was so glad I did not care. A journey started as a boy of ten ended as we entered the city gates. Here was my destiny. I wanted to embrace it.

The evangelist had gathered the Christians together for a welcome gathering. There were more than one hundred smiling faces. Suddenly I was left out. In their happiness at seeing Mr. Oleson after a year's absence they forgot me. God's gift from Manchester! They had not been awaiting my arrival but the older missionary's. Their forgetfulness was exactly long enough for God's whisper, then I was caught up in the celebrations.

There was a place for me.

I had two rooms, one for sleeping, one for study. I went out and strolled around the city as if it were home, and wandered outside the city gate. It was near to the Chinese

New Year and as I returned a man was killed in a scuffle. Mr. Oleson suggested that for the present I should not go out of the city unaccompanied.

On March 21, mother's birthday, I celebrated by giving my first address in Chinese. The lesson for the day was difficult so I told the story of the Good Shepherd. After hours of preparation, writing it out all in character and then going over it with my teacher, I preached in Chinese, and had a lovely warm feeling as I spoke, seeing from the faces before me that I was understood. Soon I was taking my weekly turn at prayers, but longing for a completely free tongue in the language.

Ten were baptised in Tsunyi in May, including an old man, his son and daughter-in-law, which meant another Christian home. About one hundred attended the services, although only seventy were baptised Christians.

My rooms were in a beautiful Chinese house, built entirely of wood for a rich family. They liked the house but when each new baby was a daughter instead of the longed-for son they decided it was haunted and built another next door, renting the first to us very reasonably. The rooms clustered round two courts, with lovely carvings and pots of flowers outside.

In September I was left alone.

The Mission sent Mr. Oleson to Anshun, and I now saw only Chinese faces, with no one who could speak English. I am not a solitary person, but these months were beneficial.

The Chinese evangelist accompanied me to the outstations, along newly opened roads recently occupied by bandits. We took bedding and books with us. The villages were showing fresh signs of life as the inhabitants returned, a few to find their homes burned or looted.

We joined local Christians in thanksgiving services, and

heard how two prominent church members had been dragged to the mountains by bandits. Following prayer both had escaped. Another had got away after jumping from the city wall. A chapel had been partly burned, another used as a hostel and desecrated by opium. It had now been scrupulously cleaned. A devout farmer, converted at seventy, went there three times a day to pray.

We moved on to find that a Chinese evangelist had been killed by bandits. It was a horrifying story. We encouraged Christians whom it had not been possible to visit for years, setting up bookstalls in market places, where the evangelist preached.

Two Australian missionaries, Dr. and Mrs. Rees, were a five-stage journey away at the capital, and I went to see them. Returning with my coolie, on the third day towards evening, I developed a severe headache. The coolie was well ahead, as I was letting the horse Dr. Rees had loaned me go at its own pace over the rough stones. I was alongside a businessman who had a coolie load of goods, when from behind a clump of trees four men with swords jumped out. One clutched the bridle of my horse and ordered me to dismount, while the others took the businessman and his coolie. As they bound my hands my horse wandered along the road and disappeared.

They took the articles in my belt – a Chinese affair with pockets – money, pocket knife, fountain pen, but threw my house keys on the ground. They bound me and the businessman to trees and disappeared with their spoil.

My companion was the first to wriggle free, and he untied me. At the next village we reported the matter and were provided with an escort of twenty soldiers with rifles for the next stage. Merchants waiting in the village tacked themselves on, but we had not gone far when we were halted by a large band of robbers covering the hillside. A soldier put aside his rifle and went forward to parley. He came back saying we would be safe if the merchants gave up their merchandise. The robbers took all their goods, and stripped them almost naked.

The Rev. and Mrs. J. H. M. Robinson, who were to be my new senior missionaries in Tsunyi, were delayed, partly by snow. I wrote in January, 1925.

> It seems to be my lot to be alone. . . The last month of the Chinese year is notable for bad weather and robberies are frequent as otherwise respectable citizens, maddened by their inability to pay their debts, turn highwaymen for the time being. I have found in Mr. Lui a truly generous soul with a single aim for the glory of God. Just to see his pained expression if he hears of a Christian guilty of meanness or ingratitude, or again his joy at hearing of an intelligent inquirer, is enough to give one hope for the future.

Twice a day I went to Deacon Lui's for meals. Occasionally on a Sunday he would invite the men in the church to a meal in his home, fostering a family spirit. I could never despair or be really lonely while there were people like him about. He was one of many Chinese Christians, I was to meet, at whose feet I gladly sat. He had a robust faith, a gentle love, and a natural courtesy. In the famine which was creeping upon us I was to lean heavily on him, and these months provided the basis of understanding and respect.

Nevertheless, I was relieved when Mr. and Mrs. Robinson came with their two little boys, John and Peter.

"You're so pale," I gasped, having forgotten the colour of my own skin.

"And so are you," they laughed.

4

FAMINE

IN SPRING 1925 WE saw the first terrible signs of famine.

The fields with growing opium were not ripe for reaping when the rains came earlier than usual, and so the paddy fields were never filled. Rice needs to be sown in water and has to mature in water. After the opium crop the fields were sealed to retain the water, but it was too late. Country people came into the city carrying coal to sell, but few could afford to buy it and the price dropped unrealistically. Rice porridge kitchens were opened.

We sent a telegram to Peking asking for relief funds. When no reply came Jack Robinson called together the deacons and we upbraided ourselves for our unbelief. We had heard God's call to help these hungry people. We must step out in faith. God had his ravens in China.

Mr. Robinson persuaded an official to give us an unoccupied temple as a refuge. The official donated one hundred dollars. We built a stove and bought utensils. The first day a dozen mothers came with their babies, the next day nearly forty, and soon sixty which was the limit of the accommodation. I cannot describe the misery as mothers, just skin and bone, tried to feed the tiny babies crying in distress. The weather was very cold and at first we had no covers for the mothers and children, but a businessman sent a pile of sacking which we stitched together. The children cried with excitement as they were tucked into the nearest approach to a bed they had seen for months.

All who could work had duties assigned to them. We built bed frames. Women fetched coal, while others made straw sandals. Each morning they gathered for prayer.

"There is only one God, he is our heavenly father, he gives us food, he gives us clothing, he continually pities us," I could hear them droning.

Deacon Lui, full of pity and understanding, went in and out, neglecting his own business, ruling by love, with a rod for offenders. A few were sick with fever and we feared an epidemic.

Finally, word came from Peking that relief was unavailable as the famine "was not caused by natural causes but by opium and banditry".

The source has failed but God is with us. We are distressed for the poor orphans on the streets. Children of five or six, with no one and no home, and some without a stitch of clothing. Many dirty, diseased and cold little ones. Deacon Lui is putting in full time. Caught snatching a bite of food I said to him, "You are really labouring." He smiled. He had found the secret of joy in serving his fellowmen through love to the Lord.

Thousands died.

Wherever I went in the city there were men and women, boys and girls, dying in the streets. I thought of the food thrown away at home as I saw bony hands outstretched. Shelters were erected as there were no hospitals and a great fire was lit to keep out the wind.

Funds now started to come through CIM and the Peking Relief Fund, but more and more hungry people flocked into the city, having stumbled over the mountainous country which surrounded us. Some never made it.

Mr. Robinson decided it would help the economy if we used some of the relief funds to buy coal at a fair price. The deacons, approving of the concept, put in two hundred dollars of their own. In a few weeks our garden became a mountain of coal, each addition being weighed. It forced everyone to give a fair price.

In the temple we had a large grindstone. Mothers ground the corn and the cereals, making puddings to sell at a nominal price with the porridge. Those who had no bowl put forward their hat or anything to hold the anticipated meal.

A cruel rumour reached our ears. It rapidly spread throughout the city. The missionaries intended to export the children to England, or America, or to fatten them for food.

"What can we do?" I asked Mr. Robinson, desperately.

"Pray," he said quietly.

Some mothers left the temple with their children, but as their places were rapidly filled with others, sickness spread among the boys and girls. The involuntary bowel movements, the constant whimpering, the brooding mothers, had a demoralising effect. We longed for Dr. Bragg and his medicine.

Eight of our number died of fever.

In the street I was accosted by a boy of ten, whose mother had died. He led me to a house where her body was on the bed. Neighbours told me the father died a few days earlier. I told them they must do their duty and see the woman properly buried. The boy joined us in the temple.

Fear struck deeper.

One of our boys was found to have smallpox. He was in

a dreadful condition, his face unrecognisable. Bandits would have caused less terror. He was at once segregated and I found a place nearby.

Now there was a drought. A play was performed at the theatre which the citizens said had never failed to produce rain. Nothing happened. Pilgrimages were made to various temples to beseech the gods for rain, the pilgrims wearing willow leaves around their heads. The shops displayed tablets, more or less elaborate, begging the water dragon to respond, and the Mandarin made state visits to temples to pray. Beggars on the streets multiplied and we squeezed one hundred refugees into our temple. The price of wheat went higher and our puddings shrank in size.

Our money will last another month. Some of the officials have promised support but have never paid. To date we have had fifteen deaths in the refuge; all but two were small children. We seem to have the goodwill of the people generally despite the anti-foreign movement.

On a Saturday in July clouds gathered in the afternoon, followed by the sweet sound of thunder rumbling, as I was called to a woman who had taken opium in a suicide attempt. On my way back, a wind had sprung up and I began to run. In a moment the street was pandemonium with people flying for shelter. Stalls were hurriedly dismantled as dust blew in our eyes, and then huge drops began to splash down.

I had some way to go and got soaked. It didn't matter. The relief of the whole city could be felt, rising upwards to meet the clouds. At Deacon Lui's I saw him look to heaven and praise God with a loud voice. Later there was a double rainbow.

It only rained for one and a half hours but it washed away the despair of a city. The clouds drifting across the sky were our happiness, and next day the prices of rice and wheat dropped. We put the last of our funds into a supply of wheat puddings.

In a few weeks there was rain in plenty, the main street becoming like a river through which we waded, but there was expectation of only half a harvest.

Although the Chinese Christians had sacrificed magnificently for the children in our refuge, twenty of the children had died.

For many months Jack Robinson had been saving for a gramophone. His family and I were musical. A missionary passing through our station had a gramophone and as we listened to two records of Ernest Lough I thought of the annual oratorios in my church in Manchester, of the big organ and the choir. Chinese interior music was not for western ears: the clashing of cymbals and loud drumming was distracting, although at funerals we sometimes heard pleasant light string music.

"A gramophone is what we want," my senior colleague would say. "Then we can hear the world's finest music."

It was to remain a dream. The money he had saved bought more puddings. After that we never mentioned the subject.

I took into the refuge a dour little boy of six, dirty and ragged, who did not know if he had a father. He was a wizen, old-man-child, whose mother and older brother had died. Deacon Lui paid his first month's board. I gave him a bath with carbolic soap, but that did not get him clean.

After some days he began to realise that I loved him. He gazed at me with his wide black eyes, puzzled by this new thing.

He became very weak with fever and stomach trouble, then one day as he recovered we saw his first smile. His face cracked and in a few weeks he became a different little fellow, singing all day long. I had spent much time with him and now felt truly rewarded. When the memories of the dead children threatened me I found healing in his trust. Whereas he used to sit and do nothing, with every tiny movement an effort, now he was constantly busy, joining me in my prayers, reminding me when I had forgotten someone.

By the end of 1925 rice was back to famine prices. A new typewriter, a gift from friends in Manchester, arrived – a real beauty, much too good for me, but sadly I had to use it to record that the tragic scenes we had witnessed the previous year were being repeated.

The city authorities opened new shelters for refugees. Mr. Robinson, Deacon Lui and I visited them. In the first shelter we found fifty people huddled round a fire. A man came to beg money to bury his wife. A little boy and girl, themselves skeletons, were sitting on a dead man's body by the fire.

We passed a temple and heard voices. In two rooms guarded by soldiers were more destitute people. So much misery in so small a place.

"We must start feeding them again," Deacon Lui said. "There'll be no relief until the wheat harvest. And that's five months."

We moved from the temple to a large house which had been in a pleasure-garden. I was appointed superintendent of the boys who would live there. The army general in the city made a donation, and the folk at home sent gifts. I acknowledged them at the end of January 1926.

The famine is getting worse. The shelters for the poor are little better than death traps. I went round to one of them to see a woman we have been feeding and she was so ill and diseased we did not know where to begin. The scene baffles description. At the door were two corpses of men, their clothes having been stolen. Rats had started to devour them. Going further in, the stench was unbearable and I beat a hasty retreat. Going to another one, I found a dead boy at the very door and no one taking any notice.

Last Thursday we had the joy of receiving another visitor into our home. Mrs. Robinson gave birth to a big baby boy, and they think of calling him James as they have a John and a Peter. In the eyes of the Chinese she is indeed fortunate to have three sons . . . but she was wanting a daughter!

Deacon Lui visited one hundred homes distributing free rice. In eighty he found they had absolutely nothing to eat. There was a heavy fall of snow and in the bitter cold more died. My boys' orphanage was full, but how could one turn away a child wailing with hunger, full of sores?

An American woman sent us a gift. She had read about the famine and decided to make her one hat last three years.

I had been spending three hours a day with my language teacher, but study, so far as book work was concerned was put aside, and I learned from the children.

A Chinese official, chairman of the famine relief in Kweichow came to Tsunyi. He was angry with the local authority. Outside one shelter he found seven or eight dead bodies being eaten by dogs. He said relief would cease unless it was put in the hands of Mr. Robinson and the Catholic priest in the old city. I was appointed an inspector, responsible for seeing the right needs were met, and that the dead were buried quickly and adequately. If this was not done the dogs and the wolves dug them up, and the crows came.

"We are not looking for more responsibility," Mr. Robinson said, "but we'll do our best."

The temperature was below freezing at night but we had only straw mats to cover the children.

Jack Robinson went down with 'flu. The children had pains and violent headaches, but there was little medicine, and no let-up from the grim reality. We became almost too tired to pray, very near breaking point.

As the gurgle of dying men rose throughout the city, fanned by the icy winds, I recalled the valedictory service and the servant who cried, "Alas, master, what shall I do?" The prophet replied, "Lord, open the young man's eyes, that he may see. And, lo, the mountain was white with the hosts of God."

I became ill on a Wednesday in February. I went to a meeting of the Famine Relief Committee in the large middle school. It was a raw day and the braziers gave out little heat. The tables were set out in a T-shape and there were long speeches about the burial of the dead and un-reliable grave diggers, and the danger of infection. I was sitting next to the French priest, getting colder and colder and becoming more and more ill.

I staggered back to the orphanage, but by bedtime I had a high fever and felt extremely ill. Believing I would not live through the night I called for the boys' teacher, Mr. Li, who was a scholar but not a Christian. I spoke to him of how salvation was not a matter of heaping up merit but of accepting Christ as Saviour. Three boys shared my room and I exhorted them to believe without delay.

"I don't know if I will live," I told them as the fever

gripped me, "but I want you to know that I will go to Heaven because I'm trusting in Jesus Christ."

"Of course," the teacher replied. "The pastor has left his home and family to come and work for God. You will certainly go to Heaven for doing this good work."

"If I only had that to trust in I would have no hope," I gasped. "You can be as sure of Heaven as I am if you believe Christ died for you."

In the morning I moved to the mission house. I could hardly walk and my head throbbed, but two or three of the older boys assisted me. When I reached the Robinsons' house I collapsed.

I was delirious and for five days remained unconscious. I grew worse day by day and my fever became so high that visitors could sense the heat without touching me. Jack Robinson washed me down daily, rinsed out my mouth with glycerine and sprinkled me with eau de cologne.

He was anxious for the children in the house and telegraphed the nearest doctor, eight days away, with the symptoms. He diagnosed typhus, but as he could not arrive before the crisis he left me completely in the care of the Robinsons.

It seemed I would die.

When the crisis came I had the sensation of falling. The Robinsons prayed and God gave them the faith I would pull through. I was sufficiently conscious to know that if God took me that I would be ashamed to meet him. I did not think he could say "well done". I was only twenty-nine.

My hair fell out but on the fifth day I regained consciousness and shouted, "Lord, save me." By the time the Robinsons arrived in my room to see what was happening I was in a peaceful sleep. The crisis was over.

Jack Robinson wrote to my parents:

You will be grieved to hear that Alfred has been seriously ill with typhus fever. About three weeks ago, I was away and on my return found Alfred with a headache; he continued for a day and then took to his bed; he got worse and worse till delirium set in and for a week he was quite delirious. I telegraphed for a doctor but he was unable to come, so we set to work to see what prayer and careful nursing would do. We had our New Year conference meetings on, and much prayer was offered for his recovery. Last Friday the crisis came and since then he has been sleeping and eating like a little child. It is all so wonderful, the rest he now has; it has been a fresh illustration to me of the rest that comes to us when we trust in the Lord. It was touching to see the solicitude of some of the Chinese Christians for Alfred's recovery. There is quite a scourge of typhus in this province and hundreds of deaths among all classes.

In his delirium Alfred frequently prayed and sang hymns, while his first request on recovery was for his Bible; your letters I have kept for him till he is a little better. I'm afraid our care has not been equal to a mother's love or a sister's attention but we have had real joy in ministering to the sick one.

I saw a man and woman carrying a man and drop him near our back gate today; fearing they were leaving him for us to bury I went to see him and was horrified to find the man still alive; on rebuking the man who had carried him, he replied, "He is sure to die."

Eight days later I was out of bed for a few hours each day but unable to leave my room. I was beginning to realise my debt to the Robinsons and to take an interest in events, reading letters and books.

On Easter Day Mr. Robinson assisted me and we went a few steps outside. My legs did not seem to belong to me, but how good it was to see the hills, the cherry and peach blossom, and in the garden the beautiful small roses I had planted the year before.

My appetite returned and I began to think of the lovely things we ate at home. The next day two parcels arrived for me. My first surprise was the size of them, and they were so well packed that I perspired with the effort of opening them.

They contained Swiss cheese, a dozen bars of milk chocolate, a tin of chocolate biscuits, tongue, caramels, candied fruits, dried pears and apricots, figs, chocolate creams, and a fruit cake.

How far they had travelled, transferred from one vehicle to another, from train to boat, and carried on the shoulders of coolies over the mountains. They were the first food parcels I had ever received.

"God allowed them to arrive at precisely the right moment," my companion said. "No good thing will he withhold."

My church had sent them for Christmas, but they came in the spring as my appetite returned. I wanted to share everything, particularly with the Robinsons, but no one was willing to partake.

"It'll make you better much quicker," they said, but it was a long process.

My skin peeled. Because we believed that typhus at this stage was highly infectious I was unable to write home, and all I touched had to be burned. I ate alone in my room. Jack examined me to see if I had completely peeled and he always found I had not.

For almost three months I was confined to my room,

while the worst of the famine passed, and food became less difficult to obtain.

That year four missionaries in our province died of typhus.

It was a happy day when I was allowed to send my first letter home.

"Oh, magnify the Lord with me and let us exalt his name together." You will have heard of the way the Lord has had compassion on me. It has been a great trial not to be able to write to you. I am taking the first opportunity, but if I write all that is in my heart this will not be a letter but a book.

The cost of living had soared but our needs were met. In my first year in China a woman who had been secretary to the High Master of Manchester Grammar School and a member of our Manchester study circle had left me a legacy of £400, which went into Mission funds and largely covered my first years in China.

Other parts were still experiencing famine. Gordon Welch who had sailed with me wrote telling how the Chinese in his province had not killed any pigs for days to see if the gods would send rain in answer to this self-sacrifice.

"Strange to say it is raining today," he said, "and the people think the gods have heard them."

From CIM headquarters in Shanghai I received counsel.

Seeing that you have had such a severe attack of typhus, it would be well for you to keep as much in the open air as possible. You will, of course, avoid studying very much, and on no account should you allow

yourself to be overfatigued. If you follow these suggestions, the probability will be that you will be as well as
ever you have been. Thank you for your appreciative
words with reference to Mr. and Mrs. Robinson's care
of you. The Lord will reward all such labours, for inas-
much as they have done it unto you, they have done it
unto him.

5

A SWISS GIRL

"ALFRED, I KNOW THE GIRL you should marry," Peter Oleson had confided soon after we arrived in Tsunyi.

I was immediately on my guard.

"Rose Piaget," he went on undeterred. "She's a lovely girl, and she's Swiss, in fact in every way suitable for you."

I looked war-like.

"I'll buy the wedding dress," he offered as an inducement.

Before the Robinsons had come to take charge, he had paid a last visit to Tsunyi to see the Christians before his furlough. On the Robinsons' arrival he suggested it would be kind to leave them alone to settle in while I accompanied him to Kweiyang. Put that way, I could hardly refuse, though I knew his aim was to bring Rose Piaget and me together.

I found that she was not only special but came from a very special family. And she was very lovely. But the will of God must be clear before anything else.

She was born in La Côte-aux-Fées, a small village, really a series of hamlets, in Switzerland. The village in the Jura mountains is surrounded by cultivated fields, pasturelands and woods, and is celebrated for its watchmaking.

"The Piaget works, holders of numbers of high awards," one writer said, "is equal to the most famous watch-making works in our country and carries the name of La Côte-aux-Fées to the four corners of the world."

Rose was born on September 18, 1894 and said farewell to her extensive family when she embarked for China with the CIM in 1920. Like myself, she heard the call of God through a missionary speaker, Louise Köhler, who served in China for fifty years with only one furlough. On that furlough Rose met her.

After language study in Yangchow she was designated to the south-west. She was escorted from Shanghai to Kweichow by Miss Köhler, discovering the difficulties and dangers; bad communications, interminable slow travel, the constant activity of bandits. She arrived safely at Miss Köhler's station at Tungchow in September 1921, after travelling for four months.

It is with profound thanksgiving that I can look back and review the road the Lord has led me. He has done miracles for me. He has sent the angels before me and protected me. He is looking after me and preparing me for his service.

In the ancient city of Kweiyang, the capital of Kwei-chow, she continued her study of Chinese.

It is tiring, very tiring to memorise these different character designs. Everything is difficult at the commencement (a Chinese proverb).

Two years passed before she gave for the first time, and all alone, a lesson to the Sunday school in her new language. Her subject was the call of Samuel: happily, the children responded. She went out selling books with her

Chinese teacher, worked in the hospital, and visited the women's prison.

In 1925 she left Kweiyang and settled at Chenyuan, seven days' walking distance, in the same province, but she found the place was swarming with robbers who menaced an unprotected population. Guns fired around the mission station and there was fierce fighting. The bandits took personal property, including clothing, and many villagers were taken as prisoners.

While I was seriously ill she was caring for forty children orphaned during the famine.

In December 1926 as a multitude turned against the foreigners on their soil thousands of missionaries had to leave China and Rose wondered if she would have to go, but she was able to stay until her furlough the following year. After a journey of twenty-nine days by sedan chair, caring for a year-old orphan baby, she took the train at Kunming, capital of Yunnan, the neighbouring province, for Hanoi and Haiphong. She reached Marseilles in September 1927, after an absence of seven years.

Volunteer missionaries came to our neglected province from Kiangsi where work was well established for a new "forward movement" in Kweichow. Among them were the Misses Wray and Twidale, who spent some months with us before moving on to their appointed field. During this time Miss Twidale fell seriously ill and I was asked to escort them the ten stages to Chungking. To save two days' travel we took a boat on a river full of rapids. During the five hours' journey, we encountered robbers twice, and most of our luggage was stolen. I was taken captive, but released after some hours and caught up with the women. With relief we reached Chungking.

I returned by another route, striking inland. This gave me the opportunity of visiting a missionary widow, with whom I spent some happy days awaiting a steamer. Then word came that I must return to Chungking to escort three women into the province. I had no idea who they were.

"It's the last thing in the world I want to do," I said, "after running two women into danger."

My view rapidly changed. Rose Piaget, back from furlough, was one of the women. Was the hand of God in this?

We were quite a caravan, the three women riding in sedan chairs. There were over twenty coolies. Before we reached Tsunyi, a coolie ran away with one of Rose's loads. The head coolie investigated and found the baskets in a wood with little left.

"Your eyes were on the girl instead of on the loads," I was later chaffed.

A Christian never enters marriage lightly. Because she had dedicated herself to God and China I knew how seriously Rose would view it. On the journey we had talked but we both had a wall of reserve. Mile after mile I thought of these affairs of the heart, resisting an impulse to take her in my arms.

Life is short, I told myself. I'm over thirty.

You are not worthy of such a girl, another voice responded.

When we had parted I had to write to her. My letter arrived when she was having a meal. Her companion suggested it was about the missing goods, so she put the letter on one side until the meal was finished.

For two weeks she pondered.

How long two weeks can be. "God," I prayed fretfully, her face before me, "if it be possible."

She sought out her senior missionary. After they had talked and prayed she wrote to me. I could hardly suppress myself as I made the joyous journey to her.

"First, my parents' consent," she said.

She showed me the photograph of her family with, seemingly, enough members to populate a village.

"This is the family council," she laughed. "Alfred, you must write."

She was not seeking a formal consent. More, much more, than that. I weighed the words, she translated them into French and together we sent it.

I wrote two letters to my family, sending one the normal route and one via Siberia.

I have asked Miss Rose Piaget to be my wife and she has consented and so we are both awaiting the approval of our parents before making the announcement public. I was alone here for Christmas . . . I was really glad. It left me quiet to pray and make my proposal to Miss Piaget and to write to her parents. How good the Lord is to give me this joy. I wish I had a nice photograph of her to send to you. I am sure you would fall in love with her too.

At the end of January I was invited by Cecil Smith, acting superintendent, to spend a few days at Rose's station in Kweiyang.

She is so lovely, I know you will just take to her. While it has been largely enjoyment, they have given me quite a few meetings to take; the main service, the prayer meeting, the street chapel preaching. It is hard to believe my furlough is just around the corner after seven years. I will be travelling by boat and that will help to modernise me a little before arriving. I will need some adjustment.

From both Switzerland and Manchester came letters of consent. I had never been so happy, but before our wedding we would be separated by a curtailed furlough. I had waited impatiently for it, now it seemed less vital. Mr. Hoste, the CIM director, wrote congratulating us on our engagement.

"You have made a wise choice," he told me.

At the end of March 1930 I received a telegram from Shanghai giving me permission to begin my furlough. By the end of April I was sailing on the S.S. *Ping Wo* down the Yangtse. One officer was from Liverpool. His broad Lancashire dialect was a tonic.

How I needed that adjustment.

The first officer was at his cabin door as I passed. I heard beautiful singing coming from inside, with a complicated accompaniment. Seeing my astonishment, he asked me into the cabin, and there I found the sounds coming from a radio, the first I had seen. The officer looked at me like something from the ark.

It took approximately forty-two days from Shanghai to London by boat, an opportunity to study French in readiness for meeting Rose's parents in Switzerland. I had not been there since I was five but had promised to see her family on the way back to China. Her father, himself a skilled watchmaker, was diabetic and blind.

The long boat journey, with the change of diet, did me good. The sunshine and wind and waves ministered to me, but I was dying for news of Kweichow and Rose. As I watched the seabirds, the flying fish and the gorgeous sunsets, I needed someone to share it with, the companionship of someone close.

We were not a demonstrative family but I had a wonderful home-coming, full of surprises, with new faces and missing faces, and a great deal that was unchanged. I was able to be with my father for his seventieth birthday; I had not wished to miss that, but there could be no settling down. China was my base, here I was a visitor.

How quickly the months went. In February 1931 I said goodbye to my people and went to Switzerland to meet Rose's family, first calling at the Bible Institute where she had trained.

Rose's father was in bed, very weak. Maman called the family together and we sat around the table. Fourteen of her seventeen children, seven sons and seven daughters, were alive, all married except Rose.

"I am losing my Rose," Maman said, unable to restrain the tears.

I felt guilty but from that day I became part of a wonderful Swiss family. Her father, chief elder of the Free Church, prayed with me, taking my hands in his.

When I reached Shanghai there were eight letters from Rose. Some had been to Europe and back again.

Our wedding day was fixed for June 10.

It was in the chapel in Kweiyang, half in English, half in Chinese, with more missionaries present than ever before in the city. Everyone stood as Rose came down the aisle, beautiful in pure white Chinese dress, embroidered white Chinese satin shoes and a veil given by her sisters. The ceremony was performed by Rev. Ieuan Jones, assisted by a Chinese elder Yeh. Chinese friends joined us for a Chinese feast. Fourteen courses for seventy people!

We travelled in ceremonial chairs to Tsingchen, an outstation eighteen miles away, for our honeymoon. These chairs were carried by four bearers, but for special occasions and for speed an extra four ran alongside and took turns, changing from shoulder to shoulder without lowering the chair. As we drew near Christians came to greet us, setting off fire crackers. It was nearly midnight before we were alone.

We were designated to Chenyuan, on the borders of

Hunan province, and there we made our first home.

Soon after our wedding we received word of the golden wedding of Mama and Papa Piaget. All the immediate family were present except Rose and a grandchild in hospital, in all sixty-one people. There were thirty-six grandchildren, eighteen boys and eighteen girls. Papa was carried down to the chapel in a chair, and was well enough to take part, addressing the assembled family for the last time. He died the following month.

The chief problem in Chenyuan was opium, where some addicts were hindered from becoming Christians because of it, but one opium smoker who had been attending our street chapel, open all day for those who could read, became a believer through the witness of the colporteur. To his distress the horrible craving remained.

"I'm a Christian and I can't do this," he told himself. He did not seek us out as we would have advised. Terrible days followed. On the fourth day when he could stick it no longer he lit the lamp and prepared the opium. As he was lying down to smoke there was painful crick in his neck.

"This is Jesus telling me not to do it," he said, deliberately putting the opium away.

For three more days he endured agonising withdrawal symptoms, then the craving almost went. In the following weeks when it returned, it was always less severely.

"I'm so free," he said when we saw him.

Although an addict thirty years, he became one of our most faithful Christians, his deliverance being a witness to the power of God.

There were discouragements.

We were pained by the spiritual state of our evangelist, a capable man. We had three days of prayer with four other missionaries joining us, and were led to pray either for his revival, or his removal. Soon after he resigned, although continuing to attend the meetings. The deacons and the members were a comfort to us at this critical period and the work was maintained through their willingness to shoulder extra responsibility.

Two hundred missionaries came to China in answer to prayer between 1930 and 1932. One of them, Gordon Smith, from Australia, was with us until he had to go to Kuichow. His days were spent studying Chinese, but his presence was an inspiration.

How China needed those missionaries. For millions life was uncertain. Executions were commonplace. I had already had four encounters with bandits. The famous trio Mildred Cable, Franscesca and Evangeline French were arrested and held for months.

"We are in a satanic whirlwind," wrote Mildred Cable.

Into this situation came two young women, Grace Emblen and Elizabeth Stair to reopen the mission at Szenan. Rose and I travelled the five-day journey with them and saw them settled in. We left troubled by rumours of robbers in the district and blocked roads. They were typical of hundreds of women missionaries who pioneered the Gospel in places where men would have feared. Years before Hudson Taylor had written:

There was nothing but the protection of God. The towns were all walled, many of them containing ten or twelve thousand people who might be and frequently were at war with a neighbouring town. To be received kindly in one place was often a source of danger in the next. But amid such circumstances the preserving care of our God was the more manifest.

There were experiences which refreshed us. Lazarus Yang, the eleven-year-old son of our colporteur attended a week of prayer preparatory to special meetings. After one meeting, reaching home, he told his father he felt unwell.

"If you've stomach ache you'd better take a dose of salts," his father said.

"Daddy, it's not my stomach, it's my heart," he replied, bursting into tears. "While we were praying, God showed me the blackness of my heart. I'm a big sinner, daddy." A confession of his misdeeds followed. "For years I've been stealing from you, and only this morning I took a hundred cash piece, out of your money bag. At school I've been wicked too, swearing and lying."

"Only the Holy Ghost could have lead my boy to humble himself like this," his father later told us. "He would never have done it had I beat him for an hour to get him to confess. When my lad finished his tearful explanation, we knelt down together and prayed."

The special meetings commenced and Lazarus was again convicted, and told his father that he had previously made only half a confession. Now he withheld nothing.

Others in the church likewise sought pardon. For Rose and myself it was a season of joy,

6

HELD CAPTIVE

OUR KWEICHOW SUPERINTENDENT called us together to pray for revival. Although tens of thousands of tribespeople had turned to God in our province, after decades of witness there were only a few hundred Chinese Christians in the towns and cities. We journeyed for ten days to Anshun to link with other missionaries. Nothing was organised, some fasted, but soup was on hand, as twenty-four of us waited upon God. A few had vivid spiritual experiences, praying through the night, and in all of us there was born a fresh vision.

Prayer had been continuing for two or three days when Rose and I arrived. It lasted ten days. A letter was drawn up, signed and sent to the churches, acknowledging where we as missionaries had failed. We had not handed over responsibility and positions of authority, we had not accepted our true role as servants, we had not waited upon God as we should have done.

I confided in Rose that God had given me a special promise during a period of quiet prayer, quoting the verse, "We are more than conquerors through him that loved us."

"And my promise," Rose said, "is 'All power is given unto me in heaven and in earth'."

We said our farewells to the other missionaries in a spirit of expectancy, conscious that the Almighty was with us, thinking of the refrain we had been singing:

I'll go with Him through the garden,
With Him to judgment, With Him all the way.

Returning from Anshun to Chenyuan we spent the last Sunday in September 1934 in Kuichow, a newly opened station, with Mr. and Mrs. Arnolis Hayman, preaching at the services. We were accompanied by Su En-lin, our cook. I spoke on the Transfiguration telling how afterwards the disciples had been confronted with the demoniac; the plain inevitably following the mountain peak; for Christ, after the glory, the agony of Gethsemane and Calvary.

In the afternoon there was a baptism and in the evening we preached in the main street before a great crowd while Rose addressed a women's meeting indoors where several signified their desire to follow Christ.

Exhilarated by the days of prayer, and encouraged by the response from the women, our Sunday with the Hayman family was altogether pleasant, and we rose cheerfully the following morning to continue our journey.

Arnolis Hayman escorted us outside the city.

"A safe journey," he said. "And go carefully."

We turned and waved. Soon he was out of sight. We never dreamed we would meet again in less than twenty-four hours in quite different circumstances.

The date was October 1, the twelfth anniversary of my sailing for China.

We had a choice of roads. The old road was longer; the other better protected by soldiers, at least in parts, so that was the one we travelled. A third of a mile from the small village where we planned to lodge for the night, as we ascended a small hill, armed men rushed from the bushes.

Rose was ahead in a mountain chair. A revolver was brandished at her.

"Don't shoot," she said. "Take what you want."

Communication was difficult as the armed men's dialect differed from that in our province, but the revolver was lowered. Robbers, she thought, after our belongings. It's happened before.

I tried to signal to her. Bound by one arm I was led down the hill. With relief I found she was following still in her mountain chair. I too wondered about the identity of the robbers, but soon they told me they were Communists, part of the Red Army, disciples of Lenin and Marx. As we descended the hill I could see people milling round the village, tension everywhere.

My heart sank. Already slogans were being put in various colours on the walls, written in huge characters, easy to read at a distance. I looked more closely. Our captors included women, hair bobbed, dressed identically to the men.

We were in the hands of the Kiangsi Communists, who allegedly had been defeated, yet were now making their way through Kweichow. They were in retreat, part of what was to become known as the Long March.

In the main body of the Red Army there were 85,000 soldiers and 15,000 supporters.

We were taken to large horse-stables where, in the best tradition of the Red Army, most of our possessions were returned, including silver dollars we carried when travelling.

If they did not want our property why had we been arrested? We were not long in doubt, being moved to a house where the chief judge was resident.

He accused us of being spies for an imperialist government. The Communist creed stated that missionaries were spies and government agents, covering up their motives by propagating religion. I told him we served only Christ.

"Who is your God to let you fall into our hands?" he laughed.

"He has sent us to tell you that he is the living God," I replied.

"You are to write letters," he said.

Together there were four: to the Swiss consul, to Mr. Gibb, China director of the CIM, to Jack Robinson, superintendent of the province, and to the church at Chenyuan. The letters asked for 100,000 dollars for each of us.

"Impossible," I gasped. "200,000 dollars!"

Nevertheless, I wrote, knowing the letters would call forth prayer.

The wife of the judge was sitting on the corner of a bed observing me. She looked as if she had been toughened by her life, but when she spoke I found her educated and pleasant. I turned to her on behalf of Rose.

"She will not be able to stand the travelling," I said. She had had a miscarriage. It had been our sorrow. "The life of the soldiers will be too hard."

"I'm also a woman," she replied firmly. "She'll have to rough it like I do."

When I told the judge and his wife of our allegiance to Christ she told him I was speaking "devil" words, her term for something superstitious or uncanny.

In the village, with thousands of soldiers in the vicinity, sleeping space was scarce. Rose slept on a narrow bed made by putting a few irregular planks together, and shared this with the Haymans' servant who had been with us when we were arrested. I tried to sleep in the only available place, an upright chair but sleep that night would have been elusive in a luxury hotel. Soldiers slept packed so tightly on the ground around us that there was no space for me. Before dawn they brought us a basket of cooked rice and a wash-basin of cabbage for breakfast, but we had little appetite for food, and before daylight the company began to move ahead. We had with us the Haymans' servant, our own cook, and four coolies. Two of them carried loads and two my wife's mountain chair minus its oil sheet awning, which had been ripped off the previous day, and divided to keep their bundles dry. It was raining as we left, and the first few miles were covered at a snail's pace.

> I'll go with him through the garden,
> With Him to judgment, With Him all the way.

The refrain went through our minds. How easy to sing.

The company was heading for Kuichow; we were returning to the Hayman's station. Seeing our destination we prayed they might have time to get away. The city was built on a hill and was difficult to enter, but when the citizens saw the thousands of soldiers they offered little resistance. Those who were not armed had heaps of stones to aim at the attackers, but they were soon overwhelmed.

The Red Army had a four-line slogan.

> The enemy advances, we retreat;
> The enemy camps, we harass;
> The enemy tires, we attack;
> The enemy retreats, we pursue.

Inside the city the Haymans warned by the chief magistrates prepared a basket and dressed their two small children to flee, but events moved too quickly. By 9 a.m. the army entered the city, and a detachment of soldiers made for the mission house where they found the family. In a short time Mr. and Mrs. Hayman and Miss Grace Emblen were brought to the house where we were being kept.

General Hsiao Keh, of the Sixth Army, the judge and two other officers, one wearing Mr. Hayman's raincoat, came to discuss terms. They told us our punishment should be execution, but as an act of leniency they would accept a fine instead. It would be 100,000 dollars each.

"Shall we let the children off half-price?" one of them whispered.

The General would have none of it.

"They are potential imperialists," he said. "The total fine is 500,000 dollars for the new prisoners."

Mr. Hayman and Grace Emblen wrote letters accordingly. When they had gone Rose announced:

"I've a message from God."

She told us how she had held on to her Bible when they tried to take it from her. Starting out that morning before dawn, she waited until there was enough light to see, then let the Bible fall open where it would. The pages opened at Psalm 124 and she read:

Our soul is escaped as a bird out of the snare of the fowlers: the snare is broken, and we are escaped. Our help is in the name of the Lord, who made heaven and earth.

The very next day our coolies were released. Now we concentrated on securing freedom for the women and children. We petitioned the judge. Eventually, he said that one of us should be held to represent each country: Miss Emblen, Canada; Mr. Hayman, New Zealand and myself, Switzerland. It was a big concession, meaning the release of Mrs. Hayman and her children and my wife. The fine remained at 700,000 dollars.

The thought of separation numbed me, but a remarkable peace filled my wife's heart. With little privacy we said goodbye behind the bed curtains.

"Are you well?" Rose asked.

"I'm fine," I replied, "but get the people to pray."

For a few seconds we clung together. I thought the separation might be for days. Rose sensed other possibilities.

"We're in God's hand," she said.

I hated to let her go without protection, but caring for the children would occupy both her and Mrs. Hayman, filling the minutes, saving endless fretting.

"If we suffer with him we shall also reign with him," Rose thought as we parted.

They returned to the mission house to find every room ransacked. What was not missing was broken. Only a few books and crockery were untouched.

"Let's tell the Mission what's happened," Rose said, but the city was in such a state there was no way of sending a message. The young manager at the telegraph office had been beaten to death, his father taken prisoner. The resourceful colporteur offered to find where the next telegraph office was situated, while they found milk for baby Benjamin. Rose wrote to my parents.

Our hearts are very sore. However, we know that nothing can come to us without his holy will. . . We pray much for Mr. Hayman and Alfred that the Lord will give them the ready answer when questioned by these evil men, and that they may be endued with all patience and forbearance. . . I trust that the Lord will have helped you to receive this terrible news as from him. He allowed Job to be tempted so much, but just so far, and it will be just so far for our dear ones.

That summer Rose had written to my mother to tell her of her miscarriage. Mother had replied at length. With the arrest of Grace Emblen, Mr. Hayman and myself, Rose was now able to view it differently.

Thank you for your very deep sympathy. I felt so very sorry especially for dear Alfred's sake. He loves children so and I could foresee how delighted he would be to have one of his own. The Lord knew what the next few months were bringing forth for us and I certainly now praise him for his wonderful ways of dealing with us. It was all in love and to spare us probably greater suffering and dangerous situations. He doeth all things well, therefore I can trust him that this present test is also out of his amazing love.

That same month, John and Betty Stam were martyred in the little town of Miaosheo. Like their Master they were led up a small hill to die, under the shadow of the pine trees. Their tiny baby, Helen Priscilla, was concealed from the killers, and carried by evangelist Lo, with his own baby for days.

Helen Priscilla Stam was brought to the CIM Home in Wuhu in December, 1934, wearing the outfit made by Betty Stam, in which she had dressed her tiny daughter on the morning after the Red soldiers broke into their town.

In her own distress and loneliness Rose ached for that little one.

When the tempter comes to worry me with doubts and fears, I must run to my High Tower, my Refuge, my Rock, my Lord.

7

AN ARMY FOR AN ESCORT

THE FIRST DAY PASSED, with long moments of intro-
spection, as we wondered when we would see our wives
again, and how we would face up to the weather, the long
marches, and our captors. They were not all cold-blooded,
happy executioners, but some were fanatics who would
take a man's life as casually as a chicken's. Ruthlessly
dedicated, with what they saw as honourable designs.

After walking five miles through the mud Grace Emblen was given Rose's mountain chair. Being a heavy girl
she was really too much for two men to carry under such
conditions, so she had still to walk much of the way. We
covered only fifteen miles that day. Our general agitation
was not shared by the guards who celebrated their victory
at Kuichow with fresh pork, seaweed and eggs, and the
spoils of conquerors, including women's woollen hats
which the men wore over their own, new shoes, gay paper
umbrellas and bedding. Star possession was a Roman
Catholic altar cloth worn as a cape.

At Whitsun in Manchester thousands of well-scrubbed
Sunday school children had marched through the city for
the annual processions, dressed in their best, with banners
and bands. It was something like that. But there was haste
and pressure, and an intensity which suggested time was
limited.

They had slogans and they plastered them everywhere, in red, white or blue. "Down with landlords, dividers of our land and capitalists!"; "The Soviet Government is China's only hope"; "Don't pay your debts to the rich"; "Religion is the opiate of the people"; "Take Chiang Kai-Shek alive." The slogans were the responsibility of an agile propaganda squad, with tins of paint and crudely printed leaflets.

We were part of their propaganda. The realisation came as a shock.

That evening Mr. Hayman and I were compelled to sit on chairs in a main village street with red strips of paper pinned to us identifying our country. While marching we had had to keep rank, and our place in the long line. Grace could not do this, so they gave her extra guards and she came as she was able. She received similar exposure in the village street when she joined us an hour or so later.

"I can bear it," I thought as the curious streamed by, commenting on our big noses, yellow hair and pale eyes which, it was claimed, could see three feet into the earth but could not penetrate clear water.

"Big nose, Hook-nose – Foreign devil – Deserve-to-die imperialists," they cried, adding to our strain. Our exhibitor beamed, as if he had created us.

"There's been a great victory over the foreigners," he declared. "Their religious society must pay a huge ransom."

The spectators multiplied as word spread of our ordeal, but not every face was hostile, and I thought of how Christ must have looked for a tender glance. Mostly, our heads were bowed as, limp with weariness, we prayed for our womenfolk, for Grace, and hoped our morale would hold.

At our resting place there was a heap of grain as a bed for the three of us, our Chinese servant and Miss Li the Hayman's servant. A small bowl of lard, with a strip of cloth for a wick, served as a lamp, burning through the night, an armed guard keeping watch in the shadows.

After the next stage I was summoned by General Hsiao Keh, himself only twenty-five, to translate a French map of Kweichow. He wanted to know all I could tell him about the roads and towns, wishing to avoid the few motor roads in existence. My conscience momentarily questioned. He was an enthusiastic vivacious leader, faith and determination bright in his eyes, his life constantly in jeopardy but he did not complain. It was easy to see why men cheerfully followed him.

I showed an assistant magistrate my Chinese Bible, pointing in the Psalms to the folly of fighting against God: "He that sitteth in the heavens shall laugh." He took the Bible and slowly read the second Psalm.

On our first Sunday we heard firing in the distance and the long column which had been almost incessantly on the move during daylight came to a ragged halt. We collapsed by the roadside and when we had gathered ourselves read Grace Emblen's *Daily Light*.

The race is not to the swift, nor the battle to the strong... Unto thee lift I up mine eyes, O thou that dwellest in the heavens . . . our eyes wait upon the Lord our God. . . O our God, wilt thou not judge them? for we have no might against this great company that cometh against us; neither know we what to do; but our eyes are upon thee.

Grace, suffered terribly, but was very brave. On that Sunday we had to retreat over a high mountain range. It was treacherous going and we rested for the night on a hillside, there being no flat ground. It was so steep we kept slipping, but at dawn we were off again, pale, nerves strained.

She found it difficult to keep a firm footing on the slippery track. If she twisted an ankle or broke a leg her life would be in danger, but she said little, keeping her energy for the mental and physical effort.

"She'll never keep it up," I said to myself. "For five miles, ten miles, yes, but this is an endless journey."

Mr. Hayman and I would have stayed with her, to show brotherly concern, but we were not allowed to break ranks, leaving her to Su En-lin and her guards to stumble over tree-trunks, and boulders.

"The Lord's giving her supernatural strength," Mr. Hayman said as the hours stretched out.

Continuing along a tiny path at night she slipped over a precipice, with a deep ravine with a rushing torrent far below. Miraculously, after falling five feet she was caught in thick bushes. Another time when she fell on the track out of sheer fatigue and fainted, the guards feared she was dead.

There were no street lamps on these mountain passes at night, so after dark we relied entirely on the guards who used bundles of bracken and sticks as torches. If they had breath the soldiers sang, but usually they had not enough to talk.

We feared Grace would die. While content to leave our destiny to God, we felt a responsibility for her. It was easier to trust for oneself.

"God," we prayed, "release her soon. Very soon."

We spoke courteously and we hoped persuasively to our guards, and the chief judge and his wife, who travelled with us near the centre of the column, but they abruptly dismissed our plea. Further effort seemed futile.

She shared with us further words from *Daily Light* for that week:

"None of these things move me, neither count I my life dear unto myself, so that I might finish my course with joy."

Anxiety was heightened one night when after we had rested for two hours she had still not overtaken us, and there was greater alarm when her empty chair was seen. Our only comfort was that our faithful cook, Su En-lin, was there. She would have his assistance if she were alive. The road was difficult but we were forced on until dawn, when her guards overtook us.

"She's been set free," they told us.

As they said this when a prisoner had been executed we feared the worst.

In fact Grace had been at the end of her strength, when the words came to her, "Stand still and see the salvation of the Lord which he will show you today." Then Su came and whispered, "Walk a little slower. I've overheard them discussing. They are going to abandon you." She slowed down. "Stand still." She literally stood still and to her astonishment the guards went on. Tired of standing she sat on a stone until the tail end of the army had disappeared, then she and Su descended the hill and found their way to a small farmstead where they stayed for two days, later making their way to Chenyuan where German Roman Catholic sisters fed, clothed and housed them.

After eleven days the Haymans' servant girl Li Kung-ching was released. Official letters were sent with her saying how the Communists now wanted ammunition, radio parts and foreign medicines instead of money. Besides these official letters we secretly gave her private letters for our wives. I had started my letter to Rose before Grace's release.

It is with hope that I can get this letter off to you soon that I pen these few lines. These few days have been a story of God's goodness and mercy to us, a time of testing his love and faithfulness. . . Dear Su En-lin is just splendid. Nothing is too much trouble for him and as Grace's chair gets behind he keeps with her and helps her a whole lot. He is truly a son of consolation. My mind just dwells all day on the love of God and how he tempers everything for us. Grace is being wonderfully sustained and we keep cheerful and seek God's glory in all things. *October 10.* A few days have gone by and we are recalling a hundred and one mercies of the Lord. My heart feels for you in your anxiety but you know where to roll the burden. Poor Grace has been wonderfully brave but has suffered very much. Now, we hear she is free but no details. We are sure Su will do his best to get her to friends and we hope she will quickly recuperate. As for us, our sufferings physically are as nothing in comparison. *October 11.* An opportunity is presenting itself to write you. Li Kung-ching is being released tomorrow. There has been fighting and retreat and silent marching in the dark but as our days so has our strength been and so it shall be. We have not been troubled with vermin and the food is generally free from red pepper. I have not the time now to go into any details of our journeys, but we have passed through most magnificent country and I can revel in all God's wonderful handiwork. Pray on and may all the dear friends do so and God will manifest his power to deliver out of the hand of the enemy. Oh! I am so glad you were spared this trial. For we who can walk it is more like a picnic. We have little opportunity to do any cooking ourselves. Mr. Hayman and I have happy fellowship together.

Miss Li had suffered savagely during her days of captivity, forced to walk every step, cursed and bullied by her guards. We had never looked upon her as a bright Christian, yet her trust in God was strengthened by her trials. When threatened with beatings and even death she did not falter, refusing to deny her faith, but her release lightened our own burden.

One night the order came for all lights to be put out, and conversation ceased as we plodded slowly through the darkness, each touching the shoulder of the man in front, feeling with his feet for the next step of the rocky path. Passing a gap in the mountain we were in danger of being seen by government troops in the valley below. Once out of danger hurricane lanterns and bamboo torches were re-lit, and the long procession, with torches whirling to revive dying flames, presented a fantastic picture in the dark.

If we could have broken away and reached those government troops; if our guards had left us so that we could have slipped into the darkness; if we had all been captured. . . It was idle, wishful thinking. To lie down and sleep, bundled up in a blanket, would have been bliss.

Three purposeful guards marched by our booth each leading a terrified prisoner. A few steps beyond us the captives were ordered to kneel. Feeling sick we turned away. A young soldier, about seventeen, wiped his sword on their garments when he had beheaded them.

We should have feared him. Oddly, he showed us kindness, even giving us a precious lump of salt, but his deed lived with us, and from that day we called him the Executioneer.

It was difficult to know if we were advancing or retreating. We moved at a rapid pace out of firing range when we met government troops, going this way and that. Being in the middle of the column we were safe compared with most comrades. We heard the rumbling and saw the smoke, and sometimes the dead and wounded, but our talk was more of food than ammunition. We reached a village in heavy rain, our misery as real as the water dripping from us. The guards in similar plight, made a huge wood fire and invited us to strip, and dry our clothes.

An ox was killed and a guard gave us a large bowl of sliced raw beef to take with us. As we journeyed our minds constantly turned to this uncooked meat. That night we put it over the fire and made a delicious stew. The guards helped us to eat it, our best meal since our arrest. For most of the time we had been hungry. Next day the man who had given us the meat returned and asked what we had done with it, apparently having intended that we only carry it for him. He was not too angry.

My shoes were nearly gone. After our feast of beef I walked almost five miles to our resting place with one shoe. I told the captain of the guard who promised to find footwear, but evidently forgot. The next morning I bound my right foot with cloth, but the judge noticed. I smiled guiltily when galoshes were taken from a comrade for me. For weeks the comrades had not rested long enough to make their straw sandals. Some cried, their feet were so painful.

I said a special prayer for the comrade, never again to take my feet or shoes for granted. In this life comfort for one is often costly for another.

Mr. Hayman and I sang hymns as we pushed ourselves along, restoring our spirits.

"What will it be now?" I would ask.

"Moment by moment, I'm kept in his love," he would reply, or perhaps, "Count your blessings."

We did that every night, mentally listing the things for

which to praise God, including our strength to "carry on". Daily we read the New Testament, no one forbidding us. During October *Daily Light* was strikingly appropriate as it recalled how God had made the sun to stand still, and had caused the iron to swim, and had opened a way through the Red Sea. Such a God was not unmindful of us. His host was surrounding us – we were prisoners of the Lord.

Twenty-seven days after being taken, we rested for one day. Twice we had walked a day, a night and a day without resting. We were now in Szechwan. I remarked to the captain of the guard that we had only three good meals; once when they killed a cow and shared the beef with us; once when we were lodged in a house which made wheaten biscuits; and on this our first rest day when we bought two pounds of honey from a peasant. We washed our clothes and took our first bath, discovering we were prey to lice.

It was a gala day for the soldiers, bands playing and banners flying, with large and generous smiles, for we had met and joined General Ho Lung's Second Army. His troops were more poorly dressed, but having the Red Flag and the colour red more in evidence. They had linked to form a stronger band; but for ourselves, our case seemed more hopeless.

"The greater the number, the more insignificant we become," we said.

There was talk of another rest at Yuyuan, in Szechwan, but we rushed through one city gate, literally ran through the street and out of the other gate. Government troops were harassing. Our weariness must have been evident for we overheard the judge's wife suggesting they should let us share a horse. For the next three days the two of us had a mule between us and a disagreeable muleteer.

We stayed in the home of a landowner where, because

he was wealthy, the soldiers took what they wanted, then summoned the peasants to empty the granaries.

"Where do you draw the line between peasant and landowner?" I asked.

"If a man tills his own soil he's all right; but if others work his land, he's an oppressor," I was told.

We stayed over a day in this place and they feasted on pigs, ducks and chickens.

A boy, accused of spying, was brought in and set to work making sandals. Occasionally, he would burst into tears and ask them to send for his mother who could prove his innocence. All day long and late into the night he made sandals, shivering in the cold – his own clothes being few as they had taken his worthwhile garments. The following day he was executed.

We were handed over to the Second Army, and for the next month were with five prisoners who were on a list to be treated with consideration. One was a fourteen-year-old boy from Pensui, the station from which another missionary, Howard Smith, was taken at the same time. He had attended the children's meetings at the chapel opposite their shop. One thousand dollars was being demanded for his release.

The Second Army did not provide us with horses as our former guards had promised, but they gave us cloth sandals which were better than the footwear we had been wearing. The first time we travelled after dark with this army, they roped us as they did the other prisoners. We rested in a farmhouse where they brought a middle-aged prisoner reputed to be very wealthy, but after months of imprisonment and hard travelling he was unkempt and haggard. He had slight bullet wounds in his head and hands received during his recapture, but these did not save him from a beating. While other prisoners were housed in a granary we were placed in a room and given a straw mattress on a wooden frame.

Our position in the army, with an armed guard between the two of us and in single file, was immediately behind the standard bearer. The flag was red with a black star, in the centre of which was the hammer and sickle. It was un furled only on special occasions. When furled it was pro tected by a canvas case made out of a waterproof oil painting of Christ's birth taken, I believe, from the Gospel hall at Pensui. On the painting could be seen the shepherds with their sheep, and the star over Bethlehem. And so we followed the Christmas star. Like the wise men uncertain where it would finally lead us!

Our roads were muddy paths and slippery stones, quagmires as several thousand men and horses tramped over them. Falls were frequent, clothes mud-caked, but not all our captors were inconsiderate. If one temporarily lost self-control the conditions were foul enough to upset the most tranquil man.

In Yungshun when the American Catholics and the Finnish Protestants escaped, they left behind English magazines and books. It was refreshing to see a book in English. For eight days we remained in clean quarters, with a bed made on a long table, high from the floor

There were five prisoners of longstanding, including a fourteen-year-old-boy, whose eventual fate we never learned, plus a woman school teacher and two girls in their teens. As all prisoners in turn were taken into an adjoining room we could hear them being questioned and beaten, and the clink of money being paid.

The mission compounds were looted, but we knew the absent missionaries would not have begrudged Mr. Hayman and myself the unsweetened milk, butter, bovril and tinned tomatoes we were given. We also bought fruit, eggs and food made with flour, and regained our strength. A Red Cross man came once to treat our sore and blistered feet.

We would gladly have stayed, but approaching government troops made us move on. Sometimes an order to move was given in the middle of the night. On other occasions we would start out and after going a mile or two would wait for half a day or so. We never knew what to expect, neither did they.

The melancholy of our guards vanished when hundreds of government troops were trapped in the mountains and taken prisoner, a victory which enabled us to return to Yungshun. As we approached the city the plain had the rubble of a battlefield.

We spent the night outside the city. There was no food and little water, but we had a tin of unsweetened evaporated milk, some butter and a little sugar and with these three luxuries made "ice-cream". This plunder had been given to us because our companions disliked anything made from milk.

After one day in Yungshun we moved towards Tayung, planning to enter the city on Saturday. By midnight, dead tired, we were still a few miles away, so orders were given to find quarters, much to our relief. The next day, Sunday, we approached the city. It was necessary to ferry the river, and again we were bound with ropes to prevent our escaping, making it humiliating for us to pass through the streets. We remained here for several days and spoke of Christ to a prisoner, a seventy-year-old former magistrate in Chekiang. Two months later he was executed.

We were given long Chinese gowns, loot from the wealthy, for the very cold weather.

Word came that the Second Army were leaving. In the middle of the night we were taken to a house of the Sixth

Army guards which was to serve as our sleeping quarters. As there was no straw to place over the cold, hard stone floor, two layers of newspapers served as a mattress for a bed in the corridor. A cold draught swept along it. At one end a prisoner was tied to a chair in a tortuous position so that he could not move. In an adjoining apartment there were a score or more prisoners. The next day there was neither breakfast nor dinner. Early in the afternoon we were roped and taken two miles out of the city. Our spirits sank.

It was a sorrowful procession. A wealthy man, who had sprained his ankle in an attempt to jump over a city wall, was carried on a stretcher by his own servants. The others, old men and women, boys and girls, numbered fifty or sixty. That night we shared a granary for a bedroom, measuring five feet by ten feet, with two other men. A bar across the room prevented us from putting our beds the long way, making it impossible for us to lie at full length. One man, over eighty, was out of his mind. Later, no respect being shown for his age, he was taken out, and bound and beaten to drive sense into him. The other was the lame man, whom we believe was later executed.

In the next room prisoners were lying with their hands tied behind their backs, crying for mercy, as they were tortured. They were forbidden to move or talk. They received two small portions of rice porridge a day – generally cold, and were given no water for washing. After being beaten, blood would remain on their faces for days. During the first few nights, sleepless because of the groaning and noise, I prayed for the peace of God in the midst of violence, derangement and hunger. It was like hell, the cries of the tortured most distressing.

Again we were asked to write letters.

Life improved when we moved on to Taowo, where we

were to remain for several months. We passed through the doors of a compound into a large courtyard with rooms on each of the four sides, and ample space for the guards to drill and play. We were separated from the other prisoners, a large room with a mud floor being allocated to Mr. Hayman and myself. The furniture was a bedframe, the springs composed of woven rope resting on stones to keep it off the ground, and when we were given straw to place on the rope it seemed luxurious.

8

AN ESCAPE

DURING THE EARLY WEEKS of captivity our fears would have been less chilly if we had known the whereabouts of our families. In fact, Mrs. Hayman, her two children, and Rose reached Kweiyang safely; but the Christians there fearing the Communist troops might soon make for the capital, advised them to go on. Rose wanted to stay in the province, but Mrs. Hayman had Shanghai in view, and Rose went with her to assist with the children. Two American Seventh Day Adventists graciously offered to take them to Kwangsi in their car. It seemed God's provision as they set out one Sunday morning covering two hundred miles that day and more than 200 the second. On the outskirts of the city they heard a shot and thought it must be the tyre, but when the driver jumped out he found a bullet hole.

Our women and the children had little clothing but at an Adventist Mission and at the Bible Churchmen's Missionary Society they were given clothes, food, fruit and 50 dollars in Hong Kong currency. There was consideration everywhere. It helped their fortitude in singularly oppressive circumstances.

From the Blind School in Canton, Rose wrote to my parents on October 31.

My heart has been longing to be able to write to you. You will be thirsty for news; alas! I have no other news but about myself to give you. I have heard nothing about our dear ones in captivity. It is today exactly a month that we met with this great trial of our faith. It is the greatest, dear parents. May our dear and faithful Lord sustain you as he does me. I realise moment after moment such a blessed and inconceivable peace which certainly surpasseth human understanding. . . When we left Kiuchow, the Haymans' station, we had just one load – weighing under a hundred pounds – besides what we had on our chairs, but we collected a good many things ere we reached Wuchow so our luggage had doubled. Again, at Wuchow, I was given two dresses which fit me like a glove. At Wuchow I mentioned about the deafness in my ear. Dr. Hayes of Canton is their dear Beloved Luke, the Physician. He is a specialist for ears, nose, eyes and throat. I have a letter of introduction. At the Blind School they have been celebrating the American Thanksgiving Day. It was all so very interesting and one was amazed at the beautiful singing. In the evening we went to a concert in another part of the city. I have not been to many concerts in my life. I thought how much dear Alfred would have enjoyed the piano and flute. The lady singer imitated the lark and was in perfect harmony with the flute. My tears rolled down my cheeks, I could not retain them for thinking of my dear husband, he loves music so.

The next day Sunday we came back to the Blind School, went to a Chinese service first, then an English one, where the preacher was Dr. Barnhouse from Philadelphia. He spoke French to me but I could hardly get a ready answer in my own tongue.

Dr. Hayes has discovered that my throat is probably the cause of my deafness. Tonsils are in a bad state. I praise the Lord for bringing me here and having the opportunity for treatment.

I am confused at the great loving kindness of the Lord. Surely he careth for dear Alfred and the others, and will not permit that they should suffer above their strength. Be not anxious but pray. It is only prayer that shall help our dear captives through and bring them out if it is God's will and in his own time.

Shortly before Christmas Rose received the censored letter I had written on December 7.

We have again been requested to write you to press the ransom for our release. We have been here over a week at this base and our great desire is that someone will be able to come to us while we are still here. We long for news of you and our Kweichow fellow-worker. You will be glad to know that Arnolis and I are both well in health and are treated as well as can be expected under the circumstances. You will realise by now that we have joined up with the Second Army under Ho Lung's command. May you be guided in all you do, my own dear one. At the same time we are writing Mr. Gibb, Hunan Province Governor, and our Consuls.

My thoughts are continually with you and of course I long for the revoir which will be granted in answer to prayer. In the meantime, do what you can to send some one. My love to all my friends, with all the love of my heart.

Our Mission was not inactive. Mr. Hermann Becker, a member of the Liebenzeller Mission, associated with the CIM, returned from furlough to learn of our arrest a fortnight earlier. He sought two Chinese Christians, men of character, ready to face death, who would act as intermediaries. Mr. Yang and Mr. Tsai volunteered, leaving on November 27 with letters from Rose, Mrs. Hayman and Mr. Becker. Mr. Becker knew General Ho Lung, who at various times had been in his study. The General's nephew had been saved by one of his mission's doctors and the General had written a letter of thanks. He appealed to Ho Lung to use his influence with General Hsiao Keh to secure our release.

His two brave messengers never reached their destination. When only two days from Communist headquarters they were robbed by brigands of their money and everything sent for our comfort. The letters were taken from them and burned, and their lives threatened. Without passports they had no option but to return.

Meanwhile, the thought of Christmas made us long for liberty. My companion had not seen four of his children for three years, but this year they had expected to be a united family in Chefoo where we had our school. In the tradition of all prisoners we contemplated escaping.

"If we're caught it may be execution," I said.

"It may, anyhow," my companion replied.

There was silence, as we thought of what it might involve, the advantages of keeping together or separating, of our physical condition and stamina. It could be a long trek, over bleak mountain trails, through the Communist lines; but it was a seductive dream.

"I think we should try," I said.

He nodded.

The back door of our room was flimsily fastened. Our guard was careless and often slipped out to warm himself by the fire in the guards' room. Every evening, before dark, they had roll-call, when the captain of the guard marked his register, lectured to the men and sang songs with them and invited testimonies. It was like a kind of family prayers.

On the evening of December 17, when they were at roll-call and our guard was away, we slipped out into the twilight. A wall which separated us from the hillside was easily scaled and a stream crossed. We could hear them singing and the sound was reassuring. The main roads were watched: the brightness of their fires glowed in the distance.

It was very cold, the moon was obscure and although we lost our sense of direction at first life seemed good under the high vault of heaven. It was when we had walked most of the night only to discover that we had come back nearly to the same place that we admitted our exhaustion. We waited in the drizzling rain and the pitch darkness and shivered for about an hour by the roadside until dawn.

We saw a house and, at some risk, made towards it, to find the occupants bewildered and frightened at the sight of us. As they listened to our story the seconds were a lifetime, but they gave us breakfast then urged us to go, saying they expected the Red Army that very day. They pointed out the safe direction. The people in the second house were very hospitable, giving us food, accepting no money and even calling us "Pastor". Yet they, too, were afraid to shelter us. Although terror-stricken, a young man was sent along to escort us on the way to a temple in which, they said, we might hide. He said a hurried good-bye and left us. The temple was barricaded against attack and we had some difficulty in finding entrance, until an old priest heard our movements and invited us in.

"Go," he pleaded hastily, fearing calamity. "They come at night to search for landowners in hiding. It is dangerous."

We were leg weary, the cold had sapped our strength, and his warning filled us with foreboding.

"Isn't it safe for one night?" we begged.

He shook his head. "They always come."

He gave us cold rice and tasty vegetables to take with us, pointing out the way. As the ground was too wet for us to lie down and sleep, we passed the hours by walking up and down in a shady place praying. Just before dark we set out again, but as before we travelled in a circle. When dawn came we were only five miles from the Red base.

"God, are you really helping us?"

We were stunned by the kindness and sympathy of local people. In one home we were given rice and eggs, but even they were eager for us to finish our meal and be on our way as a neighbour's relative was a captain in the Red Army. That day we found a small cave and slept in it, after which we pressed forward, fearing that if night fell we would again lose our bearings.

"We didn't expect it to be easy," we reminded ourselves, soberly considering our prospects. "But God is with us."

We crossed a hill and met a woman carrying buckets to the well, she ran back into her house terrified. A man came out to investigate. He gazed intently.

"Don't you remember me?" he asked.

We shook our heads.

He told us he was the relative who had visited the Red Army to negotiate for "Fatty Liao", and invited us to share their evening meal. But again there was an urgent request that we should not loiter.

"We understand," we assured them, for our presence in any home made it highly dangerous for the owners.

"As wanted men," Mr. Hayman said, "we can't really expect hospitality."

At no time in our lives had we been so wanted, but in our dismal situation we felt neither desired nor desirable, showing unmistakable symptoms of extreme weariness. As we plodded on under the grey skies we met a woman who assured us there were no soldiers in the valley below, so we went down the hill to buy straw sandals in a farmhouse.

It was our undoing. The owner knew there was a 500 dollars reward if we were taken alive. After we left he sent a messenger to tell the army of our whereabouts. Half-way up the hill he called us back.

"You're on the wrong track," he said. "There are soldiers at the top of the hill. Stay with us until dark."

We hesitated. He was too eager. Others had feared to shelter us. Finally, we yielded to the request, but soon became suspicious.

We left and again pursued the mountain path, but soon we saw men with spears running after us. There was nothing we could do. I ran briefly, then we gave ourselves up. They took the three dollars we had, also our New Testament and *Daily Light*. When we met some guards from the base out searching for us they relieved us by volunteering the information that we would not be killed.

In the camp the captain of the guard struck us both across the face, before taking us before the judge who was breathlessly angry. He put us in prison with the common criminals, each to a separate room, where conditions were unbelievably miserable. Later, we were called before General Hsiao Keh and others for questioning.

"Why did you run away?" the judge asked.

It was a silly question.

"In my place wouldn't you have done the same?" I replied, not intending to be impudent.

"You're a follower of Jesus; and he says if a man slaps

you on one cheek to turn to him the other; and if he asks you to go with him a mile, to go with him two, and here you've run away. I'm not a disciple of Jesus, I'm a follower of Marx."

He was keen to learn who had sheltered or helped us, but we betrayed no one. We were bound and placed in a room with a wooden floor, each with a small heap of straw, with bricks as our pillows, in opposite corners. We were not allowed to talk. If we wanted to speak to the guard we went through this ritual.

"Comrade, I want to make an announcement.''

"What do you want to announce?"

"Please may I turn over?"

"No," he would bark back, but sometimes gave permission.

With our hands tied behind us and our legs lashed together we were dependent on him to cover us again if we were allowed to turn.. A guard left Mr. Hayman uncovered for hours, but another came along and, seeing how tightly I was bound, without a word loosed the ropes a little, relieving the pain. In my extremity it was an act of great goodness.

I dimly pictured the scene in Manchester: the crowded shops, the gaily wrapped gifts, the seasonal music, and I thought of Rose. Before her miscarriage we had pictured this Christmas with our baby, buying his first presents.

We were brought separately before the judge, questioned at length, then told there would be a public trial in the market place.

"Now you'll see what justice by the people means," the judge said, "but be careful in answering our questions, if you wish to humour the crowd and get a lighter sentence."

I saw myself tense and anxious, then recalled Christ's promise to give his servants the right words to speak at such times. I could have peace of heart and freedom from fear. The judge would have me anxious: Christ would have me free.

"Oh, Jesus, thank you."

A thousand comrades and spectators had gathered, almost in holiday spirit. A stage had been erected, decorated with flags and paper flowers, and furnished with a table and three elaborately carved chairs for the judges.

The first case was of a landowner who had shielded other landowners. The crowd when asked for their verdict shouted "Shah" (kill). The prisoner, deathly pale, was led away. Eight prisoners in all were judged, sentenced to death, and executed that day.

It hardly gave us confidence, but Christ's words which had come to mind when I heard of the trial continued to calm my heart. "And when they bring you before the synagogue, and the rulers, and the authorities, be not anxious how or what ye shall answer, or what ye shall say; for the Holy Spirit shall teach you in that very hour what you ought to say."

The judge sat behind us on the stage as we faced the throng. He asked the questions from behind our backs and we made our answers to the people. I was asked to pronounce my full name in English and to spell it. As the already peculiar foreigner chanted these still funnier sounds, R-u-d-o-l-f-a-l-f-r-e-d-b-o-s-s-h-a-r-d-t, the crowd burst into laughter. They requested Mr. Hayman to say some of the Miao words he knew, this again affording amusement.

"Why did you come to China?" the judge asked.

"I came to tell you of the one true God and to call you to repentance," I answered to the people.

I would have gone on to preach the Gospel, but the

judge quickly proceeded with his questioning. There were three charges, namely: We had a camera and had taken pictures of strategic places; we wore Chinese dress and spoke the language of the people even to the extent of learning tribal languages to conceal our true motives; and we were preaching Christ's doctrine of non-resistance. In addition, we had escaped from prison, a capital crime in itself, so were doubly worthy of death.

When they had satisfied themselves that we were spies, the people were called upon to make judgment. A deep silence fell, then one lad shouted "Shah", and another "Ta" (beat them). The isolated voices accentuated the silence. In a state of tension the judge hurriedly arose and said that we should retire. I thought of Daniel in the den and God shutting the mouths of the lions.

When we were recalled we were told the sentence. The fine was to be raised to 150,000 dollars and Mr. Hayman was to be imprisoned for one year and I for eighteen months. My longer term was, they said, because I was the instigator. Then, too, Mr. Hayman calmly surrendered, while I ran away, and they had falsely accused me of hitting my captors.

Later the judge sent for me. The guard who had been on duty when we escaped, he said, had been executed and his blood was on our heads; we must be punished as life had been taken in vain. I was invited to choose from three forms of punishment: to carry one hundred loads of water a day, to be beaten one hundred stripes a day, or to have only two hours' sleep in the twenty-four. As I did not have the strength to carry the water and the other two would mean death, I did not choose, but told him that if he would give me something which I could do I would willingly do it. However, it was only an idle threat.

We were troubled about the guard, and had been

anxious for his welfare when we escaped, but he was later seen alive and cheerful!

The silence between Mr. Hayman and myself was rigidly maintained. The day after our trial was Christmas Day. Memories tumbled in, the sounds, the sights, the goodwill, the smells, and our mouths watered. Judging from our outward circumstances there could not have been a more dismal day. The weather was cold, there was no fire and our sole pastime was sitting in our corners on the floor, the monotony only relieved by three meals of rice and vegetables eaten in silence. But our Lord sent a message to me in one word: "Emmanuel" – God with us.

The day brightened and the walls widened.

"Emmanuel." I longed to pass it on to Mr. Hayman, but how? Then the idea came to form the letters in straw. And so, unknown to the guard, it became a message of cheer to my companion also. And, knowing we should be imprisoned no longer than he would allow, we rejoiced in tribulation. Joy broke over us and sweet relief. God was with us.

The judge summoned us and told us we could choose between continuing our strict imprisonment and paying a fine of a dollar a day for the imprisonment period.

"We have no money," we replied, but assuming we would eventually pay he relaxed our conditions.

"We cannot give you as much liberty as before you escaped," he explained, then required us to write further letters which said that for two anti-aircraft guns they would reduce our fine considerably.

We trudged back to our prison, now to converse but only in Chinese. When the guard overheard me whispering a prayer in English with Mr. Hayman he made us sleep "head and tails" Chinese fashion, and this went on for months.

On New Year's Day, also my birthday, I asked God to speak to me, and his words came in the thirty-seventh Psalm: "Oh, rest in the Lord. Wait patiently for him, and he shall give thee thy heart's desire. Commit thy way unto him and trust in him. Fret not thyself because of evil doers. Oh, rest in the Lord." The aria in Mendelssohn's 'Elijah' echoed in my mind.

On the wall we wrote "A.D. 1935." The guards reading the figures understood it meant the year, but what did the letters mean? Explaining about "The Year of our Lord", gave us another opportunity for witness. The Communists did not use the date from the commencement of the Republic of China, but our Christian date, thus subscribing as it were, to the Christian era.

Other prisoners were treated more harshly, and those who tried to escape were usually beaten mercilessly, the guards taking turns in administering the stripes. Bamboo instruments of torture were put on special prisoners at night and taken off in the morning. Those who died from starvation, ill-treatment and sickness, were carried out and buried uncoffined like dogs. Two women came to negotiate for the release of a very old man – a relative. After being detained for a few days, they saw him being carried out for burial with hands and feet tied to a pole as pigs are sometimes carried to market. At one period it was almost a daily experience to see prisoners, men and women, led out for execution; sometimes the men were stripped to the waist, sometimes barefoot but always tightly bound. Seeing all this it was apparent that God was restraining their attitude to us.

I dreaded the monotony of prison life. A prisoner, a delinquent Red soldier sharing a room with us, was unravelling a pair of socks.

"Why are you doing this?" I asked.

"I want to make 'ears' for my sandals," he replied.

As a child my mother had taught me to crochet. When released the prisoner – who had not used the wool – offered it to me. I obtained a crochet hook by shaping one end of a chopstick with the guard's sword. Because we had no shoes I first made a pair of bedsocks for Mr. Hayman, the guards watching the curious process with astonishment. They brought me wool to make into a cap for the company trumpeter, and from then I never lacked an occupation. Orders came for caps, gloves, mittens, belts and jerseys, until there was a waiting list, everything made in the only stitch I knew.

On Sundays I put all work aside, observing the day of rest. It was easy to remember the dates, as we prayed for the provinces assigned each day in our CIM prayer list. On Sundays they themselves did not drill, but cleaned their guns and did odd jobs.

One memorable day, through the partition, Mr. Hayman overheard the judge speaking of "the running dogs of the foreigners".

"I think someone has come to find us," he said.

9

THE EXTREME PENALTY

IT TOOK "THE RUNNING DOGS" fifteen days to reach us, hiding from bandits and soldiers, crawling on all fours to avoid detection, passing skeletons and beheaded bodies.

They were the three volunteer messengers sent on January 25, 1935, by Mr. Becker, to negotiate with the Red Army for our release. Messrs. Chai, Yang and Ho, all Christians, knew they were putting their lives at risk. In the mountains the snow was a foot deep, making the views breathtaking but their steps treacherous. When rheumatism in Mr. Yang's feet crippled him so that he fell behind, he was tempted to return, but they prayed and continued, typical of the finest Chinese brethren willing even to perish themselves.

Their exhaustion was so apparent on their arrival at our camp that they were allowed to rest, meeting us on the second day when we were given censored letters from our wives. It was an occasion of high excitement. For four and a half months we had received no word. We had not known what had happened after our parting at Kuichow. Our worst fears were quickly dispelled, and there was the happy confirmation of Grace Emblen's release.

Our world was suddenly a place of extraordinary beauty. We stumbled to find the words to thank the mes-

sengers for making the perilous journey. They saw our
feet were bare and on leaving, after an hour's supervised
conversation, in an extraordinary act of Christian charity,
took off their shoes and stockings and gave them to us.
We had steeled ourselves against hardship: against such
an act of friendship we had no defences.

On February 16 the messengers left with letters for our
wives, and a frightening letter from the Communists, ae-
manding anti-aircraft guns to be delivered by March 15
besides 100,000 dollars, and much medicine, to reach them
by April 14. If the guns, money and medicine failed to
arrive we would be killed.

In vain our wives had written in January to General
Ho Lung and General Hsiao Keh.

Dear Sirs,

We have not hitherto communicated with yourself or
other officers, as it seemed to us scarcely fitting for
foreign women to write to you, but in view of the special
circumstances we feel that we must send this letter to
you.

It is with no other reason than to do good and to show
kindness to the Chinese people, especially the poor, that
we have come to China. Neither have we at any time
acted in any way adversely to the interests of any class
of people, our hope being to show kindness to all at all
times.

It is now more than three months since General Hsiao
Keh came to Kuichow in the course of military opera-
tions and took us captive. We are grateful that he was
willing at that time to let us and the children go free.
We are very pleased also that our husbands, Messrs.
Hayman and Bosshardt, have stated in their letters
more than once that they have had kindly treatment

and consideration during the time of their captivity. But we would remind you that for months their wives have waited anxiously for their release, and Mr. Hayman has four sons who are grieved and sorry that they have not been able to see their father whom they expected to meet at New Year Season. We are not in a position to demand that they should be set free, neither is it in our power to make any promises of ransom or reward, but we would appeal to your kindness and generosity, who also are fathers, that for the sake of the women and children who have been long separated from their loved ones that you will give orders to your officers to release our loved ones at once and let them return to us. And we shall invoke a blessing on you and kindness in return for this shown to us.

Yours faithfully,
Rhoda Hayman
Rose Bosshardt

Much of our waking hours was spent in prayer and in the recalling of Scripture passages and hymns. We were able to remember about five hundred of these in whole or part. As a memory aid we would repeat as many passages as possible on subjects like sacrifice, holiness, love, long-suffering; first selecting those beginning with "A" then "B" and so on. Relaxed moments were spent going through the names of Bible plants, animals and proper names alphabetically.

We had no clock, but in our darkened room, where we were kept for six weeks, with a ray of sunshine which shone through a small crack in the roof making a circle on the opposite wall, we could estimate the hour from eleven in the morning to three in the afternoon. The room was shuttered to keep our whereabouts secret.

Being next to the captain of the guard's room, we overheard the questioning of new recruits.

"Why do you want to become Red soldiers?"

"Because we do not have enough to eat at home," they invariably answered.

Towards the end of March the entire Red army prepared to slip away from Taowo where it had made its home for some months. Soon after midnight we were brought our breakfast, gathered our few belongings, and joined the soldiers stealthily gliding away like a long snake in the darkness, not saying a word. It was uncanny.

When we reached Lungchiachai, a market town, new quarters were established. The two of us were assigned a granary for a prison, so small that we had to put our bed diagonally across the room. Through an opening we had a view of the courtyard and the beautiful scenery beyond, part compensation for the smallness of our accommodation.

In every place where the Red army halted for any length of time a place was selected as the Lenin Hall. It was both reading room and a library of sorts. As there was no suitable room here they constructed one, of straw mats supported by eight poles for a ceiling, and evergreen branches suspended on bamboo poles for walls.

After five days a messenger came with pen and ink, requiring us to write more letters, dictating what we should say. Before we wrote he told us the mind of our captors concerning us.

"The fine must be paid within the next month. If it is not paid by May 9 you will receive the extreme penalty."

We smiled uncomfortably. It was the first official threat of execution.

The next morning we moved on with the army. Until now we had always had someone to carry our load – a travelling rug, flannelette sheet, patch-work quilt, wadded coverlet, extra clothing and shoes. We ourselves carried a haversack containing bowl, chopsticks, toothbrush and other odds and ends. But now we were to carry our own things; we each put one rug around us, and made the rest into a large bundle, taking turns in carrying it.

"I'm going to faint."

For the first time, apart from stomach troubles, I was ill. Struggling up a hill towards the end of the day I had the first hint of heart strain. Although I had earlier known extreme pain in the calves of my legs after a long march, this was more serious. The guard became concerned and the bundle was taken from me, but during the next days I was so exhausted that I repeatedly fell to the ground.

Our heavy winter clothing was needed at night, but was too warm during the day and so had to be carried. Finally, because of the difficulty of keeping up with the rest, we threw some articles away, including a wadded gown.

"They won't need to execute me in May," I told myself one terrible night, when my tense body would not rest. It was my worst hour. The next day I was forced to go on, never before so close to defeat. My legs would not hold me, and in desperation I cried to the captain of the guard to take his revolver.

"Shoot me," I said. "Shoot me."

My endurance had gone. With only a month to go, I might as well die a little earlier. Rose and my family would understand that living had reached an unbearable pitch.

He did not shoot. Instead the guards became more considerate, using milder terms in urging me on. But once when I fell down they dragged me into a field and left me. Being semi-conscious, I heard them return and say, "He's alive, he's still breathing."

They prepared a stretcher and found two men to carry it, but I managed to walk. We were to have rested in a landowner's house, but after laying down the judge called everyone into the courtyard, where he said there had been a great victory. We were to proceed immediately to the place of conquest.

For the most part I rode a horse for the next days, developing a high fever, and an acute pain in the side of my chest which Mr. Hayman massaged. So critical was my state that the guard asked me what I would like to eat. When I mentioned some citrus fruit we had seen on the street, he gave me large oranges, very expensive, sweetmeats, and a bowl of meat dumplings.

As the day fixed for our execution drew near, Mr. Becker was very active on our behalf.

On March 25, Mr. Yang, Mr. Ho, with Mr. Hsiang from the Evangelistic Band, started out for further negotiations. Mr. Tsai had been obliged to drop out. The first five days they met robbers twice, but were not attacked. On the day before they reached the Communist lines, a band of robbers tied them up, threatened them with death and took the letters, food and clothing which they were carrying. Finally, two were released but Mr. Yang was taken off to the mountains. After six days he escaped, but the attempt to reach us failed.

Mr. Becker now found a volunteer named Job. Dressed like a beggar, carrying a little outfit for mending shoes – his former trade – he set out. After two weeks he was back. Suspicious soldiers had refused to let him through their lines.

On April 19 Mr. Ting arrived at Mr. Becker's with letters from the Communist leaders and ourselves. Mr. Becker was somewhat relieved for a few days before "eye-witnesses" had reported our death, and the location of our graves. Mr. Ting also brought bad news. The letters confirmed we would die if the fine was not paid in full by May 9.

On April 21 Mr. Ting returned with a letter to the Communists stating that their demands were impossible. He arrived in the camp on May 3, bringing with him the CIM *Monthly Notes* in which we read of the martyrdom of John and Betty Stam. It gave us cause for grave reflection.

May 9, fixed for our execution, was the anniversary of the Haymans' wedding. With the Psalmist and the Apostle Paul Mr. Hayman and I repeated, "For thy sake . . . we are counted as sheep for the slaughter."

Around the world friends of the CIM prayed, knowing that God was neither defeated nor handicapped by distance. A *Daily Mail* reporter attended the prayer meeting in Union Hall, Manchester, on the eve of our death-date.

To pay any part of the sum demanded would mean that every missionary in China would be a potential source of income to bandits. The mission dare not take this risk. It is hoped that the bandits' threat to murder the captives was bluff. . . One after another the members of the congregation stood up to speak. The remainder sat with bowed heads, people of all ages drawn together by a common bond – their belief in God and their love for Mr. Bosshardt. Occasionally a muffled sob broke out. Men's voices quivered, women found their eyes suddenly obscured by tears.

Even while a multitude prayed God was answering prayer. The judge called us on May 9.

"This is the day we fixed for the money to come," he said. "It hasn't. But we realise that Shanghai is far from here and maybe your wives have not had time to get the money to us. We extend the time to May 30."

Our families did not know. The period of waiting was almost unendurable.

We were moved from place to place, crossing rivers – by ferries, pontoon bridges, stepping-stones or wading – scrambling up hillsides, often so wet that we longed for the fire at night to dry our clothes. Sometimes we had no breakfast, sometimes we ate well. We were introduced to General Chang, of the 41st Regiment, who had been captured with two majors and a thousand or so soldiers. After this Communist victory General Ho Lung ascended a stage to address his men. When he saw us he said in a loud voice:

"Unless you pay the fine quickly, we will chop off your heads. Don't think your beards will save you; I killed a foreigner with a beard many times longer than yours."

With his flat hand he tapped the back of his neck to make his meaning clearer.

We were exhibited before the huge gathering as two foreign spies. Later, Chiang Kai-Shek's general and the two majors likewise.

I was making a garment for Assistant Judge Liu, and as we were moving he was anxious for it to be completed quickly. When he came round to check on progress our fellow prisoners said: "It's Sunday. He doesn't work on Sundays." Very angry he railed at us for our superstition, as he termed it. "If you insist, I will finish it," I said. He did, and the garment was finished, but the next day he gave his clothes to a prisoner to carry: the prisoner escaped and he lost his cherished garment.

May 30 passed and we found ourselves still alive, but our wives and families did not know. As early as March our death had been reported. Then the news seemed so reliable that Mr. Warren broke the news to Mrs. Hayman in Shanghai and word was sent to Rose in Chinkiang. That weekend they believed they were widows, but on the Monday morning fresh telegrams seemed to indicate that the news was not true, and within a few days they had proof of this from Mr. Becker's messengers who had talked with us for one hour.

Now they were again in suspense.

On July 1 the Manchester *Daily Dispatch* carried a report from Peking.

The British Embassy has received further word concerning Mr. Hayman and Mr. Bosshardt, missionaries captured at the end of last year. On June 17 Chinese saw two foreigners at Lichia in Hupeh – they are thought to be Mr. Hayman and Mr. Bosshardt.

In fact on May 30 the Red Army had more important matters than two weary missionaries. They were besieging a city. Being so near to the actual fighting we could hear the firing of guns. While aircraft dropped bombs, we found protection in natural caves on the hillside.

We rested for a month or more, giving our feet a chance to heal. For my festered little toes I made an effective poultice of hot rice.

The judge was now very angry.

"Mr. Becker is only playing with me," he declared after calling us before him. "Fancy offering us $3,000, when we require more than that from any small landowner. You must write and tell him to gather together as much as possible and send it along as quickly as he can. We will give him just fifty days in which to get it here."

It was not the occasion to remind him that Mr. Becker's offer was not in payment of a fine, as we had been wrongly accused, but in payment for our food and the inconvenience they had experienced in taking us along.

After a pause he continued: "Upon second thoughts we will give him until the end of next month (August), which will mean a little longer."

"And what will happen if the money does not come by then?"

Again we noticed his hesitancy. "If it doesn't come then you will be executed – at least one of you will be."

We wrote the letters, but a day or so later were asked to rewrite them omitting the time limit, but adding that if our middlemen came again without any money at all that they would treat them as spies which would mean imprisonment if not death.

We silently noted his new attitude: the large amount of the fine was no longer mentioned, the time limit withdrawn.

During our time in the Lungshan district a girl comrade of sixteen or seventeen was added to the company. In her younger days she had attended a Gospel hall where women missionaries had taught her to knit. I was surprised how sweet and clean she kept. She carried her kit as the men did, ate with them, and slept in the same room (they always slept fully dressed), but like the judge's wife she somehow avoided becoming coarse.

"Your middlemen have come again," we were told They had brought letters from our wives and Mr. Becker. The judge ordered us to translate everything into Chinese. Mr. Becker was now offering $6,000 for our board, and promising to deliver the money personally if the Communists would choose a "no-man's land" as a meeting place, bringing us in exchange.

I read my wife's letter, written on the anniversary of our wedding. She quoted our wedding hymn: "My heart is resting, O my God."

"Shall I translate this poem?" I asked.

"Yes, everything."

There were snapshots with the letters. Two photographs of Mr. Hayman's children, one of my wife, and a fourth of my parents. A letter of thanks to Mr. Becker from my mother was also enclosed. What joy to see her handwriting again. The judge kept all the letters, but allowed us to take the photographs.

"Pay the money quickly and then you can be free," the comrades said when they had seen a glimpse of our family life.

The judge stipulated that in our reply to Mr. Becker we must embody three points: One, We must confess that we were spies and as such should not have come to China, and that therefore the heavy fines were justified; Two, We had done wrong in trying to escape and had thus only further incriminated ourselves; Three, We were to assure our correspondents that when the money was handed over we would be set free. We were also to enclose a list of medicines which Mr. Becker was to purchase and deliver. We tried to avoid the full force of the confession that we were spies by using the phrase "as spies."

We returned to our room.

Judge Wu sent for me, a dictionary and the letter to my wife before him. Glaring at me through horn-rimmed glasses he ordered: "Translate the first part of your letter."

"Is this the proper word for 'spies'?" he questioned. I found it in the English-Chinese dictionary before he would believe it.

"What does this word mean?" he asked, pointing to "as". "Why do you say *as* spies? You *are* spies." He told me to write clearly that we *were* such.

"I refuse to write that as it is a falsehood," I replied.

He became beside himself, and shouted so that all could hear.

"You *are* a spy. When you were judged there was ample

evidence proving you to be such. If you are not a spy, why did you come to China?"

"I came to China to preach the Gospel," I repeated. His face turned paler.

"If you are not a spy then why did you have a camera?" he bellowed.

"I had no camera," I answered.

"Why have you purchased land in China?"

"We have purchased no land in China."

"I command you to write this letter as we say," he thundered.

"The letter is to my wife and she knows that I am not a spy even if I am made to write it," I persisted.

"I don't care to whom it is written, you must write it according to our wishes or we will execute you immediately," he threatened; and I could see the hatred in his heart.

A member of his company escorted me back to our building, waiting until I had written the letter.

"You'd better do as the judge wants, he has a very bad temper," the young man advised.

"Now have you done it properly?" he solicitously inquired as I handed the finished letter to him. Upon being assured he took it back to the judge.

That afternoon we met the messengers in the judge's house, but as the judge was present our conversation was restricted.

"I have a copy of John's Gospel in Chinese," one of the messengers volunteered, when he learned we had no Bible. "Would that help?" Alas! Judge Wu waylaid him as he returned with the precious gift.

"You must give it to me. I shall inspect it, and if it is all right I myself will give it to them," he said. We never saw it.

Judge Wu was still dissatisfied with our letters. He now

wrote them in Chinese and had us translate them into English. On the morrow the messengers left with them written to his satisfaction.

We had long talks with the captured General Chang about the Christian faith and he asked many questions. When we told him that we believed we would be released when the $6,000 came he shook his head.

One evening after we had gone to bed Judge Wu sent for us. We hurriedly dressed. As we went through a large door leading into the courtyard we could see the Communist leaders seated in a circle; General Chang was with them, and there were two vacant chairs for us.

"We want you to sing," the judge said, "but I warn you not to sing any of your sacred songs."

Unfortunately, Mr. Hayman had forgotten his false teeth but it was too late to fetch them.

"We've practised nothing but hymns," I explained.

There was an awkward pause.

"Oh, well, sing anything you like," said a diminutive woman, wife of one of the leaders. Together we sang the hymn, "I am He that liveth, that liveth and was dead." We sang the chorus first and then the stanzas – "I am alive for evermore" – the guards standing in the background listening.

"Yin puh tso," (nothing wrong with the harmony), commented Chairman Liu as we finished. Chairman Liu was often the guest of Judge Wu. We returned to our room but we could hear their hilarity far into the night.

"By the way, what's happened to Liu? I haven't seen him for some time," I said to one of the guards a few months later.

"Don't you know?" he whispered. "He's been executed."

"What for?" I asked.

"He was a counter-revolutionary."

10

FREEDOM FOR ONE

IN A NATION OF MILLIONS, plagued by famine and war, our existence or otherwise was not significant. The local Red army commanders with many sick and wounded, with rations low, and few medical supplies, might have saved themselves further headaches by executing us, for our presence at times had a disturbing effect.

We took each new day as a gift from God.

Now as we watched through the window we thought we saw two middlemen, Mr. Ting and Mr. Tao, in the room on the opposite side of the courtyard. We waited to be called in to read the letters, but hours crept by and nothing was said, days passed and nothing happened. Despair was extinguishing our tiny ray of hope.

Our middlemen were apparently living in the guard's house and at length we saw them in the stuffy dugout where we sheltered from the bombs. We edged towards them. Afterwards the judge ordered us to be searched and forbade us to go to the shelter in future.

The following Sunday as we sang the *Te Deum* and other hymns we were interrupted.

"Judge Wu wants to see the younger foreigner," a guard said.

Judge Wu was sitting with his students. I faced him,

the students behind me. Mr. Ting and Peter Kao were seated on his right, their faces frightened.

"Why hasn't the money come?" the judge demanded.

"I don't know," I replied. "We're dependent on our friends."

He became enraged. "Strike him on the face!" he commanded the guards standing by my side. I was almost knocked over.

"I denounce you as a spy," he roared, "and you are worthy of death." Turning to the students he continued, "Now we'll punish this imperialist like the British punish our poor people in places like Hong Kong." Turning to the guards standing near me he ordered: "Strip him!" The buttons were torn off my gown, and someone spewed a mouthful of cold water on my back. My muscles tightened.

The youth who had escorted me and another young man held my arms. The thought of Christ being scourged for me and not only scourged but crucified came to me before the first stroke. They were administered with a thin bamboo with notches every four or five inches. I kept my head down. It was all but intolerable. I kept thinking of the Crucifixion.

"If it be possible. . ."

But I was so conscious of God's presence during the beating that no sound escaped me.

Judge Wu's words broke the savage silence.

"You're not laying it on hard enough," he said.

The strokes came heavier. My body winced and twitched with pain, then Judge Wu stepped from his elevated seat, and took the bamboo. I would not cry but wondered when it would end.

"How soon can you get the money?" he demanded.

"It's not within my power to say," I weakly protested. "We've always written the letters you asked."

"In my absence you sent a letter from Sangchih which did not pass my censorship. You likely wrote something in that letter to Mr. Becker which prevented him paying the fine."

The middlemen, who had witnessed my agony, exhorted me to name a date. As Mr. Becker was now only two or three stages away, I suggested ten days.

I was dismissed and Mr. Hayman summoned.

"Don't allow them to speak," the judge ordered. I prayed they would spare him the brutal treatment.

When we later shared our experiences I found he had undergone a similar ordeal. They brought pen and paper and ordered him to write to Mr. Becker, giving a fortnight for the money to be paid.

Our backs were bleeding, but I had read how slaves after beating used to wash each other's wounds with salt water to hasten the healing. On the fish which they served us that night were little lumps of salt, which we dissolved in hot tea and applied to each other.

The young guard who had held me during the beating came with popcorn, showing his concern, but never once mentioning our ordeal.

The next day Judge Wu asked me to translate an article from the *Hankow News*, an English newspaper. As he opened the paper the first bold line that caught my eye read THE WORD OF GOD: underneath was a Scripture verse, "Cast thy burden on the Lord and he will sustain thee. He will not suffer the righteous to be moved." As we had been so long without a Bible it was like the very voice of God. Later I told Mr. Hayman. If only the one who placed it there knew how God had used it to uplift his dispirited servants.

A week passed before we were asked to translate Mr. Becker's letter, in which he mentioned his perplexity.

While he believed the Communists would release us for $6,000, others doubted their sincerity. If he brought $3,000 would they release one of us? If so, then the other $3,000 would follow immediately on condition the second captive was released.

The Communists replied that our beating was to be repeated every day if the money did not come. Further, they were not doing business that he should bargain with them; to let only one go would be impossible for military reasons. The money was to be delivered in the district of Sangchih. We both signed the letter.

We were now allowed officially to see the middlemen, who were hopeful that Mr. Becker would be able to send the money, and that soon we would be free. General Hsiao Keh called to see us.

"I know you can find the money," was his parting word.

Because of constant bombing by government troops the headquarters were moved back to Sangchih, two or three stages away, over mountains and through valleys. We made the steep ascent in the intense heat of the summer sun. Among the prisoners were women, including an older woman, who painfully and slowly climbed with her guard. We were parched with thirst, but local children brought a bucket of water from a stream, more precious than gold.

While we rested the old woman jumped down a steep slope. The guard followed her, dragged her up and forced her on. Pushing and pulling her when they arrived where we were sitting, she collapsed in a heap, gasping for breath. They could not drag her much further, and as there was still a half-day's travelling execution was proposed and unanimously favoured. Three or four wrangled for the swordsman's privilege, but the eldest of the hagglers, a youth of twenty, carried the day. Borrowing a sharp sword he dragged her away, followed by a second comrade with a hoe. Soon they returned smiling, as indifferent as though they had killed a chicken for dinner.

In the heat neither of us was well, both having stomach trouble. In Sangchih we were led to the offensive room which had been previously condemned. The weather was hotter and the mosquitoes more numerous than on our previous visit, but when Assistant Magistrate Wang visited us he was so disgusted that he arranged another lodging.

Mr. Hayman dare not eat steamed rice, and it was difficult to obtain suitable food. He was given the left-over gruel from other prisoners, and this was sometimes sour. It was distressing to see him thinner and thinner day by day. As we were taking a bath, a rare luxury, on the drill grounds, the comrades noticed his protruding bones, and this led to better food.

The middlemen returned with letters, various Christian magazines, and Mrs. Cowman's *Streams in the Desert*.

We were told to write that our captors would reduce the fine from $750,000 to $10,000 which was another way of saying they would not let us go for $6,000.

"Your friends will surely be able to collect such a small amount as $10,000," they said.

The messengers seeing our weakened condition promised: "We'll bring the money as quickly as possible. Mr. Becker will be able to get this amount."

Our hopes rose, although there would be problems in bringing such a sum through bandit-occupied territory.

In a room opposite ours there was a slightly demented woman of about fifty. As she had received rough handling, and had been unable to wash her wounds or to dress her hair, she was a sad spectacle. Another woman imprisoned in a room with twenty prisoners, gave birth to a child. We heard no cries from the infant and later learned that it was dead.

For a period we shared a room with two other prisoners, Mr. Keng and Mr. Li, who wished to learn about the Christian faith. Mr. Li, who knew a little English, learned two hymns and requested that I write the Lord's prayer in Chinese for him to memorise. On Sunday they asked us to tell them a Bible story. Perhaps they saw something of the peace that God imparts, and so desired to learn more of his Gospel. They were sure our captivity was coming to a close.

The middlemen returned, with two tins of milk for us, medicine, and a dollar each. In the letter which they brought, Mr. Becker promised to bring the medicines through and $10,000. He asked detailed questions, to avoid possible loopholes through misunderstanding. We urged the middlemen to tell Mr. Becker to bring the money on November 16. He must on no account fail. We longed and expected to be with our wives for Christmas.

As we noticed that preparations were being made to move, our prayers became fervent that God would deliver us before more journeying. Mr. Hayman, unable to walk, was even too weak to ride on horseback.

By November 17 the delegates had not arrived, but we were confident that they would come on the morrow. On the 18th we were sitting by the mouth of the dugout when one of Judge Wu's men came for me. We knew by his countenance that the money had arrived. As I walked along with him he chatted freely, and I saw he was unarmed.

"You'll soon be free," he confided, leading me past the judge's house to the quarters of the hygiene squad. Judge Wu was coming out, but gave no greeting. I was asked to check a list of medicines. A doctor's wife, who was present, likewise assured me of our freedom. Peter Kao confirmed the money had been paid, and that two mountain chairs had been sent for us by Mr. Becker who was waiting at Yungshun, two days away. When the task of listing the medicine was finished, I hastened back to share the facts with Mr. Hayman. We were almost tasting liberty.

"Now for our discharge," we thought exuberantly as we were summoned before Judge Wu.

"You'll be able to go back to your friends and live like aristocrats," the guard chatted as he escorted us along. I was carrying Mr. Hayman on my back, as with swollen legs he was unable to walk even a short distance.

As we waited in an antechamber we prayed, then Judge Wu called us in and we noticed his unpleasant look. He gave us articles which Mr. Becker had sent for use on the road – a towel, Chinese face-cloth, and some aniseed cake.

"The money has come, but it's only enough for one," he said, and so convincingly did he say it that for a moment I believed him. "We've decided to release the older foreigner."

I was stunned.

Mr. Hayman begged him to reconsider his decision and let me go, but the judge replied: "You're ill and need attention. You must leave today. A chair is waiting. You'll be able to make several miles before dark."

It was a situation we had not contemplated, and we stared at him blankly. In our captivity there had developed a togetherness. Was this a bad joke? Mr. Becker had sent not half but the whole $10,000 and now they demanded a further sum. It had been delivered in silver, four coolie loads, about 400 lbs. Peter Kao had told me that the full amount had been paid, and were there not two chairs waiting for us? We had been cheated.

"Mr. Becker has gone to so much trouble to get this, that there is no hope of a further $10,000," I said.

"Your friends didn't send this; it has come from Chiang Kai Shek, and he'll send as much again. Don't we have spies everywhere, and didn't his men escort the money and as good as hand it over to the guards?" the judge said (it had been paid by a Chinese who wished to remain anonymous).

God's voice whispered to me, "I am with you always. I will never leave you nor forsake you." When Mr. Hayman turned and said, "How can I leave you alone with these men?" I immediately answered him, "I will not be alone. God will be with me." I was able to comfort him with the comfort with which God was comforting me.

The judge warned that I would be shot if I tried to escape. I read the distress in Mr. Hayman's eyes. How differently we had imagined this day. But for his family I believe he would have stayed to save me facing the winter alone.

I was led away and did not see him go. When I reached my room, the guards looked in astonishment, as though seeing a ghost.

"Haven't you gone?" they asked, then suddenly they were ashamed and knew their officers had broken faith. "What will you do without your friend?" they asked.

"I have a Friend who will never leave me," I replied quietly and they knew I was talking of the Lord Jesus Christ. It came to me forcibly that I could always count on his presence.

Mr. Hayman was led slowly to the alleyway where the chairs and coolies were waiting. He was given a passport, but when it was later scrutinised it was found to be made out for one day only. On the second day soldiers tried to recapture him but they arrived at the motor road minutes after he had left.

Mr. Becker received the news that only one prisoner had been released by telephone on November 19. It was a crushing disappointment for him, he had negotiated for a year, and for the Chinese messengers. He later wrote:

> I could not sleep that night; the disappointment was too great. I had done all I could do, and had taken every precaution possible, and the Communists had broken their promise and deceived us. On the 20th, I left after breakfast on muleback to meet the missionary, not knowing which one I would see. About four miles out I saw Mr. Hayman coming and the empty chair. It was very hard for me to see him alone, and he himself could not restrain his tears.

He cabled the CIM in Shanghai:

Hayman released, is very weak. Bosshardt detained. Leaving tomorrow for Changsha.

Mrs. Hayman was travelling to Shanghai with her youngest child when she heard the news of her husband's release.

Rose had lived on tiptoe, expecting to receive similar tidings any moment. She had been disappointed when negotiations broke down in August. Her calendar verse for that day had read: "Hath God forgotten to be gracious?" and her heart voiced the same words. Then a friend brought her the leaf of a calendar of the same date which said, "The Lord will do great things." These verses came to mind again when she heard that Mr. Hayman was free, but that I remained a captive. She was reminded of the experience of David, in Psalm 42: "Hope thou in God; for I shall yet praise him who is the health of my countenance."

> Our magazine *China Millions* said: What a joy for them (the Haymans) to spend Christmas together after the long months of suffering and privation for them! With all our hearts we praise God who has heard the sighing

of the prisoner, and preserved one who was appointed to die. Let all who have prayed for him – and there must be thousands throughout the world – give thanks to God, and ask that he may be fully restored . . . But our heavenly Father will not misunderstand if our thanksgiving on the receipt of this news was not as unqualified and exultant as we had hoped. For what poignancy is added to our concern for Mr. Bosshardt by the knowledge that he is now shut off from all sympathetic companionship. The sufferings which two might face are doubly hard for one to undergo alone. Newspaper reports that the Red army is on the march, moving perhaps to districts where it will be still less easy for Mr. Becker to maintain contact, are not reassuring. But our God is able.

Mr. Hayman reached Shanghai on December 2. Mrs. Hayman and Mr. Gibb, the General Director, welcomed him at the wharf. When he entered the Mission Home at Shanghai, weak and emaciated, and stood among his fellow-missionaries, Rose was there. There was a moment of tension as hearts were torn between joy at seeing him and sympathy with Rose.

"Shall we all sing the doxology?" Rose said, breaking the tension.

Alone in her room, she knelt by her bedside and cried, "No one can comfort me . . . but thou, O Lord." Without opening her Bible the word came to her: "Ask and ye shall receive, that your joy may be full."

"I will go on asking," she decided.

11

*A SPECIAL
CHRISTMAS CARD*

I DID NOT HATE MY CAPTORS. If I was ever tempted to feel
bitter it was when I considered the anguish of Rose and
our families, never greater than now. When life was hardly
worth cherishing I thought of Rose and the madness went
from my mind. When looking at my captors I would say
to myself, "Christ loves you and died for you," then it was
easier to love them myself.

When Mr. Hayman had gone I picked up *Streams in
the Desert* and turned to the Sunday reading: "Hear what
the unjust judge saith. And shall not God avenge his own
elect which cry day and night unto him, though he bear
long with them? I tell you that he will avenge them
speedily."

My companion had left for me a dollar and some cop-
pers, plus the towel, face-cloth and cake which the messenger had brought. While taking stock of my material
possessions I discovered that the dollar in my haversack
was missing. I recalled how some of the tin of milk had
disappeared.

The captain of the guard was unsympathetic. I told the
boy I suspected: "You'd better own up and give it back,

and no more will be said; if not, things may go ill with you." He vigorously contended his innocence.

"Maybe it fell behind the bed," he suggested. No sooner had he said it than he stripped off his tunic, crawled under the bed, and came out with the dollar.

As the boy had no bedding I shared my bed with him that night, but before dawn he was called and given his liberty. In *Streams in the Desert* for that day I found the words of Freda Hanbury Allen.

> Blessed is he whose faith is not offended,
>   When all around his way
> The power of God is working out deliverances
>   For others day by day.
>
> Though in some prison drear his own soul languish,
>   Till life itself be spent,
> Yet still can trust his Father's love and purpose,
>   And rest therein content.

About 4 a.m. breakfast was served. Again we were on the move, but it was a relief to leave Sangchih with its associations and get into the country. During the afternoon I had an attack of malaria, making it impossible to keep rank. I had quinine and a guard gave me smelling-salts which proved effective. The captain, concerned about my illness, again promised me a horse, and shared with me that night a room which had access to a blazing charcoal fire. We left at dawn, but as the horse assigned to me still had a half-load of paper, I was able to ride only five of the twenty-five miles.

Aircraft followed us, but did no more than take observation. The next day they swooped repeatedly dropping bombs as we lay beneath the trees in an orchard.

"Are you frightened?" I was asked.

"I have an unseen Friend who protects me," I explained, more conscious of the rheumatism in my left limb than the bombs.

"Tomorrow your horse will be relieved of the paper, so that you can ride it more," I was promised.

They kept their word, but the captain of the guard was unwell and asked me to allow him to ride for a while. I willingly consented. In such bleak conditions captors and captives have much in common. At the frontiers of endurance men cling together. Under extreme conditions there is a common struggle for survival.

The road was narrow and winding. Suddenly we heard "Help." Rounding a corner we saw that slippery boulders covered the steep slope from the path to the cataract below. A thorny hedge bordered the water's edge. The captain's horse had slipped down the incline, but had been caught by the thorny undergrowth at the foot, the captain still astride.

"It's a good thing the captain is on the horse instead of you," my guard said, it requiring much effort to rescue horse and rider.

I had thought the same.

My own state was not improved when the horses had to wade a stream. Before we reached the far side I was soaked to the waist, likewise the bedding on the saddle.

In the city of Supu the comrades tore down the posters left by the People's Party, substituting their own. Landowners were held for ransom, the post office looted, and mandarin oranges from a local orchard shared among us. From a Roman Catholic church was taken a figure of the crucified Christ with outstretched arms, and crown of thorns. Making fun of it, they hurried to show it to me. "Do you worship this?" they asked. I told them that my Saviour was not on the cross, but alive.

"Why should he have had to suffer so? Why does he wear a crown of thorns?" a more serious group came later to inquire.

"Our Lord himself was sinless," I said, "but the sins of the whole world were laid upon him, yours and mine."

For eight or nine days in the evenings I executed orders for crochetwork. When about 4.30 one afternoon Judge Wu gave orders for us to break camp rapidly, I could only snatch my haversack from the nail in the wall. My book of daily readings was in the bag, but the periodicals, changes of clothing and bedding had to be sacrificed, and the wool which was my raw material.

They tried to hurry me, but the pain in my limbs made it necessary for the guard almost to carry me along. Instead of marching in single file, the road now presented a mass of jostling men and animals. The criminals and captive landowners were taken with us, bound with ropes.

We had narrowly escaped being trapped by government troops and heard firing as we left the city. Eventually we filed into a field to form ranks, everyone knowing their place. The discipline was wonderful.

As our journey continued the weather got colder, with night temperatures below freezing. While climbing a mountain we came to a sheet of ice where riders had to dismount. The higher we went the thicker the ice. When the horse was taxed to its utmost, I prayed God to strengthen the animal under me.

Sleet fell but a kindly guard gave me a lined Chinese garment, thick with patches, but so acceptable. We came to a bank with a rapid-flowing river where the working squad threw a pontoon bridge. Not many days later we arrived at a large town, where the judge's secretary came and asked me to write two brief letters, one to Mr. Becker and one to my wife, asking for $10,000 to be sent with all speed.

That afternoon a Chinese doctor, a captive of the Red army, gave me a hypodermic injection, and medicine for my rheumatism, and I began to feel better.

Sleeping in the open my clothes were sometimes frozen stiff and the horse's mane bristled with icicles in the early dawn. The tall grasses were encrusted with ice. It was better to be on the march along the steep and slippery slopes, than to lie stiff and cold. Beneath the heavy grey sky and in the bitter wind events and days became hazy. Weak comrades dropped out, some died, their reserves exhausted. Men who braced themselves with the dawn shivered as the day wore on, as much from lack of sleep as from the cold. Our minds were dulled and threatened with the strain.

I hoped that Christmas Day would present relief or surprise. Perhaps I would be given the letters which Mr. Ting had brought some weeks before, or we might rest. We started out as usual about dawn. The day itself was bright and sunny, and as we climbed up the mountain we encountered snow and ice. About noon we halted and I took time to view the beauty of the scene; the skies a bright blue, the fields below carpeted with pure white, the trees blanketed with snow and ice. Half-way up a distant hillside was what might have been a Swiss chalet. Suddenly the thought came: "This is your Christmas card. And it was made by God."

That evening in a small cramped shed, put together so that draughts were not excluded, I sang carols. It came forcibly to me that our Lord had been born in a stable. I sang from my heart, "O come to my heart, Lord Jesus, there is room in my heart for thee."

The following day we came to the motor road, a thrilling sight, the first modern road I had seen since my arrest. We hurried along it for nearly ten miles, too exposed for their liking to aircraft attack. We were now in a populous part of Hunan, passing through large market towns, coming to familiar territory – I had travelled this road from Kung-kiang to Yuanchow – so at last I had my bearings.

We passed near a CIM station. The Christmas decorations had been torn down, remnants left in the street. In the village the comrades were congratulating themselves it was likely we would spend the Chinese New Year in the large city of Yuanchow, with good clothes and luxuries to plunder. But my thoughts were of the mission compound there, with the schoolgirls and orphanage, the hospital and large chapel which seated over a thousand people. Had the missionaries remained? We had official news that the city had fallen.

Five miles away we could see the city pagoda, and with this the guards became more excited. But as we drew nearer shots were heard. But believing the news that the city had fallen I prayed against reason, having an inner urge to do so. When we reached the river bank and saw the city on the opposite side, a halt was called. The vanguard were also taking shelter in suburban houses, and here we waited.

Then we turned inland and I knew – the city had not fallen! Members of the Liebenzeller Mission (associated with CIM) were in Yuanchow for protection, so that twenty-seven missionaries, including Mr. and Mrs. Becker, were gathered there. Later I learned that they were in the midst of a baptismal service when the first shots were heard, but continued with the service. The Communists were eager to arrest Mr. Becker, which is probably why they gave Mr. Hayman a passport for only one day. There were also several priests and nuns at the Catholic compound. Prayer availed and all were kept in safety. The city was surrounded for five days, but just as the government troops inside decided that they must open the gates the Communists unaccountably withdrew.

We again crossed the Yuan river. As we passed through more villages and cities my immediate longing was not for freedom but for rest; "A few days, Lord, in one place."

The guards, realizing that my home was in Kweichow, eagerly asked: "Have you been in Shihtsien?" I told them of the springs, where the water was as hot as one could bear it. They questioned my word that hot water came out of the earth. When the city first came into view it looked like a model, nestled away in a gorge, but instead of entering it, as we had hoped, we passed the gate and turned on to the busy market street along the river where most business was done. As we passed the house of a Christian woman, I strained my eyes unsuccessfully to see her.

We billeted in a house not far from the little chapel in which I had often preached. That evening Mr. Li and I slept on a bed, and Mr. Keng slept on a bench eighteen inches wide, in clean quarters. About midnight we were awakened. As I sat up and rubbed my eyes I saw a Catholic priest. We shook hands, and then the guards awakened Mr. Keng and ordered him to sleep with Mr. Li and me on the bed, giving the priest the bench for a bed that night.

Father Kellner, of German nationality, had as his sole kit two travelling rugs. On the bench he had no option but to lie stretched out like a corpse. For the remainder of the night my sleep was fitful, and I envied the way in which he slept \so peacefully on such an uncomfortable bed. The next morning he told me that really he had not slept a wink. His companions had evaded the oncoming soldiers, but regretfully he had delayed a minute or so so to hide church treasure.

"I have as much right to believe in my religion as you

have to believe in Communism," he told Judge Wu when called before him.

"If you say another word about religion, I'll have you shot," the judge retorted.

As we filed along the street, down to the riverside, I saw a dejected-looking group staring hard at Father Kellner, directly in front of me. Turning round, he whispered, "They're some of our Christians," but in no way did he acknowledge them fearing they might suffer. I turned again to look at the group and saw their tears.

My guard noticed them.

"What do you want? Clear off!" he ordered, but they followed afar, and drew near as we lined up on the riverbank.

As we travelled the priest, who had been in China only two years, noticed that I had no handkerchief. As he had several, he gave me one, apologising that it was not clean, but to me it looked snowy.

The next day, the weather still cold with snow-storms, my horse was required for a sick man, so towards the end of the stage I was very weary. As we were about to make the ascent of a steep hill, Father Kellner offered me his mule.

Late that night a captive woman was placed in a small section of our granary. An inquisitor came to question her, and when she did not answer satisfactorily, he bared her back and beat her in our presence. It was hard to endure.

Before arriving at Shihtsien I noticed three messengers from Mr. Becker. My heart lifted. As they were warming themselves by a neighbouring fire, I beckoned them. Mr. Yang told me of the deliverance of the missionaries in Yuanchow during the siege, and assured me they would soon complete negotiations for my release.

I told him how while still in Hunan, being without a Bible, I was constantly on the lookout for a portion. One day I picked up a page from the Chinese edition of Acts, containing parts of chapters fourteen and fifteen. The message to me was: ". . . and exhorting them to continue in the faith, and that we must through much tribulation enter into the kingdom of God." A few hours later I found a leaf from a smaller edition of Acts containing exactly the same portion.

A few days before the Chinese New Year, in Niuchang, we were given a room in a wealthy man's home. Glutinous rice dough had been prepared which after toasting was very palatable. There were blocks of sugar with a flavour something like that of maple sugar, stolen from a sugar refinery. The comrades had so many slabs each, but became thoroughly sick of it and gave us as much as we wanted. We had an elaborate Chinese bed, a lacquered brazier, access to a kettle and pan, and as much charcoal as we wanted.

I was called before Judge Wu, to whom Mr. Yang had been pleading for a reduction of the fine.

"A tremendous reduction has already been made," he said. "$10,000 is the least that we will consider. On the other hand we have some favours to ask of Mr. Becker and if he will accommodate us by granting these, we will pay him. If he does it well, we will make a reduction, and if he does it very well, there will be a still further reduction."

The four propositions were: First, Mr. Becker must apologise in the name of CIM for the strong letter he had written, suggesting they had broken faith with him in releasing only one prisoner; second, when the middlemen returned with the money they must be accompanied by General Chang's delegate; third, two letters must be delivered to two influential men in Kwangsi, and their replies brought back by the delegates; fourth, Mr. Becker must purchase some articles, a list of which was enclosed in the letter. If the money expended in securing them exceeded the amount of the fine, it would be credited to Father Kellner's account.

A rough draft of this letter in Chinese was given to me to translate as my reply to Mr. Becker. The demands were impossible.

When the priest came back from his interview he was also depressed by their proposition, but we wrote the letters and the delegates took their departure.

When we lodged in an inn in the town of Tsatso the landlady treated us like guests instead of prisoners.

"You've lodged here on a previous occasion," she commented and I nodded.

"In happier circumstances."

In Kiensi the city photographer was called to take photographs of the guards. I had borrowed a fountain pen, but feeling it was an indispensable item for the photograph, the owner rushed up to reclaim his treasured possession.

In Tating, where more prisoners were added to our number, we were taken to the Roman Catholic compound and placed in the gate-keeper's room with other prisoners. There were pleasant surprises in store. A little girl brought me a copy of the CIM Report *Our Magnificat,* and a guard gave me a package sent from Kweiyang, containing a pair of woollen socks, a sweater, chocolate bars, bouillon cubes, a tin of milk and a small package of coffee. Father Kellner shared my enjoyment.

We were moved to a temple. It was here that Joshua, a tribal man who had been sent as a go-between arrived. I had previously met him at Kweiyang. He was my first precaptivity acquaintance. His home was thirty miles away, and he was a bright Christian, employed as a servant by the missionaries in Kweiyang. I thanked him for the package he had brought although half the contents had been confiscated.

12

FREE!

MY CONSTANT THOUGHT HAD BEEN OF FREEDOM; when at last it came it was something of a shock. The weeks immediately preceding it did not prepare me.

We were moved into the regular prison of the yamen at Tating, a brick building with well-barred windows. For added security a cage-like structure had been built within the four walls, the bars being of timber about five inches apart. In the centre of this structure a carpenter sectioned off a portion for the priest and me, with the appearance of a cage within a cage.

I was reminded of the Chenyuan prison which we had visited regularly. The stench, the bars, and overcrowding had haunted me then.

"How can prisoners live under such conditions?" I had remarked to Rose. "I couldn't."

But through God's grace, and realising that I was his prisoner, I found myself able to bear it.

The priest had been ill and now had no appetite for rice. He had prepared men for death, now he believed he was within its shadow. A cough which I had developed, since a night on the hillside, was quite distressing. We sat hunched in our gloom. A doctor paid us occasional visits and sent us some coffee.

On this Long March, while men fought and struggled for survival, a baby girl was born. When General Ho Lung took the child – his own – in his arms he was gentle as a woman. He sent a messenger to me with skeins of good-quality wool, with German labels, probably loot from the Mission House. There were many colours: black, brown, green, purple, white and various mixtures. I was to make garments, inner and outer, for the child. I could mix the colours as I wished, making the garments in any style I chose. When I requested a pattern, I was given one for a short inner Chinese gown, and one for a long semi-foreign overcoat. I made a paper pattern and, with a beautiful crochet hook of stainless steel which he gave me, set to work.

"Who are these for?" the guards asked.

When they heard, I had a new prestige, but with such an exalted job it was disconcerting to be interrupted to take shelter from aircraft.

"Can you finish by tomorrow?" I was asked one day, which suggested we were about to break camp.

I worked late, sitting near the bowl of oil with an improvised wick. About midnight I stopped, the garment unfinished. A fever on top of my cough made the hours until reveille restless, leaving me barely fit for the road.

While eating breakfast, about four o'clock, the messenger collected the garment and the wool. We lined up in the courtyard, ready once more to march. During this and the following day I was very ill with fever, and a frightening pain in the lower lobe of the right lung, probably pleurisy. So acute and severe was the pain that I could scarcely refrain from screaming out. The nights were terrible. Due to the pain and shortage of breath I sat up. There was quarrelling among the prisoners, and the priest, though sympathetic, could do little to relieve me.

From now as it was difficult for me to take many steps, I had to go by horseback. Despite the guards and hostler constantly predicting an early death for the noble creature, God kept it moving. I prayed a lot and ate little.

Judge Wu arranged for a doctor, who prescribed some Chinese medicine, including the ingredients dried orange peel and liquorice, all stewed together.

In a small city high among the mountains, across the border in Yunnan, we slept in a loft, a family storeroom, the light coming through cracks in the walls or roof. The floor was covered with small potatoes and the woman of the house gave us permission to use what we desired.

On the road again, we travelled through wild country, spending half a day climbing a hill, wondering if we would ever reach the top. The jaggedness of the jutting rocks, and the ruggedness were indescribable. The priest was so exhausted he had no appetite for the coarse food, and became too weak even to ride his mule. The guard insisted he did so, but after an attempt, propped up by them, they improvised a stretcher. Six of the stronger prisoners, in twos, took turns to carry him. For three days these underfed carriers suffered much.

After travelling for a week through this rugged country, with snow and ice, we arrived at the border city which we had occupied a week before. Daily we were pursued by aircraft as we now journeyed into Yunnan in a south-westerly direction, taking cover repeatedly so that often night fell before we halted for a rest, which usually meant going to bed supperless. For days in succession we had only one meal, mainly of corn.

March 21, the first day of spring, was mother's birthday. We were still in the mountains with winter around us, but as we made the great drop in altitude we found ourselves travelling through a beautiful plain where the fields of vivid yellow mustard checkered the fields of beans and wheat. There were fruit trees in bloom – peach, pear and plum. I longed to send home a picture of this exquisite panorama of Spring with a birthday greeting. Softly I sang:

> Heaven above is softer blue
> Earth around is sweeter green!
> Something lives in every hue
> Christless eyes have never seen.

We lodged in a market town called Yangchang, meaning sheep market. The conviction that we were in a Methodist district was confirmed when at one stopping place where there was a post office, I was called to translate newspapers, including an English Methodist paper, but they refused me the loan of this.

We were now dismounting our horses a dozen times or more daily because of aircraft, then waiting for the bugle call which was the all-clear.

"How are you?" General Hsiao Keh asked me after approaching unexpectedly with his bodyguard.

"My cough's somewhat better, but my limbs are weak," I answered.

"We have decided to differentiate between foreigners in future," he said. "You're a Swiss citizen, and Switzerland is not an imperialistic country. You have no unequal treaties with China, neither have you any concessions, so we've decided to free you tomorrow."

"We will not release the priest," he went on, turning to where he was sitting within earshot. "He's from Hitler's country, no friend of Communists."

Father Kellner came and congratulated me. I told him that as they had once broken faith with me I would not rejoice until I was free.

"Did you understand what the General said?" I asked.

"Mostly," he replied, shaking my hand. In that moment I knew better how Mr. Hayman had felt when he was released and I was left.

It had come so suddenly that I hardly knew what to think. Recalling how treacherously they had dealt with me formerly, I was afraid to be too elated, but it was after all the General who had spoken, in the presence of his own men, within the hearing of guards and prisoners. I was warned not to think of a literal "tomorrow", but should take it as meaning shortly.

The next day it was whispered that we were going to Kutsing, where there had been a CIM station. It had been vacant for a few years, so I felt confident that no missionaries would be in danger.

It was a long hard mountainous stage, in the strong wind difficult to maintain one's position on the horse. Even in the valleys we encountered such dense clouds of dust that comrades veiled their faces with handkerchiefs. Yunnan lived up to its reputation – the Chinese spoke of the Yunnan wind, the Kweichow rain and the Szechwan sunshine.

We arrived at Chungkiai, a populous village, where we rested for a day.

"General Hsiao invites you and the priest to dine with him this evening," a messenger announced.

A royal or presidential invitation could not have been more stunning, but there was no problem about what to wear.

"I suggest that you clean up a bit," the messenger urged.

"We've no other garments," I said.

"Communists don't stand on ceremony," he replied, and left us.

The General acknowledged our arrival with a jerk of his head, and bade us to make ourselves at home, so we sat on a low stool round a charcoal brazier, waiting for the meal to be placed on a low square table. More guests arrived, including General Chang.

There were ten at the table made to accommodate eight, so two of us sat at the corners. General Hsiao questioned the priest about German military tactics. Turning to me he said, "Switzerland has no standing army, so of course you had no military training." This spared me the trouble of an explanation that might have been misunderstood.

Towards the end of the meal the General said: "We quite intend to release you tomorrow."

Another army leader by the name of Wang confided privately: "It possibly won't be tomorrow, but when it is convenient."

When the guards arrived to take us away, we bowed to the company, thanked our hosts, and trudged back to our prison. The guards were now deferential.

For two nights we travelled by moonlight, resting in snatches during the day. Marching, we were in peril of being bombed; hiding, we were in danger of being over-taken by the infantry; so that immediately upon the departure of the planes we had to scramble back into position, perhaps only to take shelter again within the course of minutes. We passed several groups of Red soldiers preparing to check the advance of the pursuing foe, while the main body ran to safety, but we seemed to get no further from the staccato of the guns behind us.

Once, because of my almost useless legs, I had difficulty in dismounting and mounting the horse, so the next time a plane appeared the groom led me under a tree so low that I had to crouch on the horse's back.

On April 11, we sighted Tawan in the distance, making a detour along narrow ridges between rice fields at different levels. It was difficult for the animals to keep their footing, and my horse fell throwing me into the mud a few feet below. I wanted to walk after that, but the groom insisted that I ride as he did not want me to break rank.

As we neared the village a messenger was waiting for me.

"We are going to release you. Judge Wu wants to speak to you."

Acting as guide he led me to the house where his company was preparing to rest. It was noon and the judge and his wife had arrived a few minutes previously. My painful efforts to dismount caused them some amusement, but as the guard was leaving me, the judge said, "You'd better take him to his room and let him rest awhile. I'll send for him when I'm ready."

In an adjacent house I was taken up a ladder to the loft where I found Father Kellner sitting on the bed. About two o'clock the guard aroused us for the midday meal, and an hour later the judge sent for me. Full of anticipation I began to collect everything I could carry, but the guard advised: "You needn't bring anything with you."

"I'm having some trouble with this Petromax lamp," the judge smiled. "Could you help me put it right?" The lamp was new, and the box contained directions in English, French, German and Italian, but not Chinese. I translated the directions into Chinese, but as he was using the wrong oil, after a while we put it aside.

The judge sent his orderly to invite General Hsiao Keh, General Chang, and old gentleman Chou to a feast.

The Red leader, Wang, was again sitting beside me. "When you report to the newspapers you must remember we are friends," he said. "You've seen how good we are to the poor, how we work on principle, and are not common bandits as we are slanderously reported to be."

"We shall be glad to hear from you if you care to correspond," said the judge.

"I've no objection to you remaining in China as a visitor," the General added, "and shall even permit you to have a school if you will only refrain from drugging the scholars and populace with this belief in God. But I think it would be better if you went home and stayed there."

When the General had gone, I made a request to the judge on behalf of the priest.

"If you want him to live until the fine weather comes, see that he receives better care. Could you not give him an orderly as you have done for General Chang?" I asked. "Someone to get him water to drink and for bathing, to provide fuel for a fire, and straw for a bed."

"Impracticable," he said, but promised to see that the orderly N.C.O. got him proper attention.

Three of us were to be released.

"You will be taken to the house of a commoner where you must stay until dawn, then you'll be free to go," the judge said. "We move shortly after midnight, but you musn't start before dawn."

He read to me a paper stating the conditions of my release. It was to the effect that I was guilty of preaching the Gospel, and that they released me on the condition that I would not transgress again. Once more they referred to Switzerland's non-imperialistic outlook as the reason for setting me free. I was not asked to subscribe to anything by either signing or verbal assent.

"I'm ignorant of my whereabouts," I said.

"It's fifteen miles to a city which is only a stage from the capital. You could arrive there in two days," I was told.

I was given ten silver dollars to pay for food. It was now ten o'clock. He told a guard to escort me to the loft and to inspect anything I was taking.

Father Kellner was already asleep. I awakened him and

left five of the dollars with him. We kissed each other, and mutually confessed and forgave each other's shortcomings. I had already promised that I would do all I could to further his speedy release.

Reaching the street, we found the messengers and a guard waiting to escort us to the house where I was to stay until dawn, but we had been resting only a short time when we heard stirrings in the camp. The bugle calls of the various companies sounded, the crunch of much marching outside our door, and there was talking and a confusion of voices. Eventually everything became quiet. We remained in bed until dawn but I did not sleep much, my heart singing praises to God.

At dawn we were alarmed to hear the door pushed open. Two grooms from the Red army closed it silently behind them. Shivering with fear, they begged to be allowed to accompany us to the capital.

Wang and the runaways went ahead and I followed slowly behind with Joshua. It was a beautiful, sunny morning. The road ran alongside a babbling brook, with well-wooded hills to the right. Joshua said how he had prayed daily for me, and told of his experiences in getting through the Red territory. He was suspected of being a spy and his life had been in danger. I expressed my gratitude, but he made light of the difficulties, reproaching himself because he had not now found any conveyance for me. Then seeing I could not make it he asked me to sit and wait while he went to arrange for men to carry me.

"Before you go, Joshua, do you know what day it is?"

"No," he replied. "Is it Sunday?"

"Yes, but a very special Sunday," I smiled. "It's Easter Day. Don't you think it's wonderful that these men who've so often taunted me that Jesus is dead, that he could not help me, that these men who said I would not be free until the last cent was paid, should have unwittingly set me free on Easter morning."

We rejoiced together.

No wonder the birds were singing. Easter Day! The resurrection morn! Jesus alive for evermore!

Joshua hurried to a farmhouse to fetch a chair in which I could be carried. I was alone. It was wonderful – delivered from the vigilance of the guards. He eventually found a man who was willing to carry and who went to find a companion. Joshua returned and insisted on carrying me on his back to the farmhouse for breakfast.

I was very comfortable in the locally constructed mountain chair, and as I was little more than skin and bones the men were not over-taxed. It was well into the afternoon before we sighted the city. At the gate we were met by a group of government troops, who questioned us and searched our belongings for almost an hour. We were referred to another officer who took a dislike to Joshua. He commanded a squad to take us through the streets to the General, marching in single file, guarded by soldiers with fixed bayonets. They thought, with my beard, I was a Russian spy.

We went through the imposing gate of a temple, breaking in upon the General and his officers at their evening meal. On catching sight of me, the General hurriedly advanced.

"Oh, you're the Swedish gentleman who has been held captive for so long," he greeted me.

"Swiss," I corrected.

"I'll see you are taken safely to the capital tomorrow, but we must find a place for you to sleep tonight."

"There's a Gospel hall where he might spend a comfortable night," someone suggested.

We were escorted to the Pentecostal Mission. The woman in charge seemed to be distracted.

"I can offer you no hospitality, as the Reds ransacked the place yesterday, even taking the shoes from my little girl's feet, and now every room's occupied by soldiers, even the kitchen," she said.

After a while she became calmer and told me of her sorrows. The guard that brought us demanded a receipt for our safe delivery. As she could not write she had to find a neighbour to do it for her. She found us a bundle of straw, putting us in a small room where the firewood was stored, where we made our bed on the ground.

We were up with the dawn, and shared a bowl of water with some soldiers to wash our faces. While so occupied Wang returned, and offered to find coolies for me. He had been gone a short time when a messenger arrived inviting Wang and us to breakfast.

After breakfast I was asked if I would prefer a horse or a chair for the thirty-mile journey. I chose a chair. We were given a special bodyguard. Half-way we stopped for the mid-day meal, and rested again five miles from the capital. Of course, no one would know of my liberation, and I knew the missionaries resident there only by name. On arrival I would ask to be directed to the CIM home. Like a liberated Peter I would surprise some Rhoda.

We had proceeded to within four miles of the city, when I saw three foreigners riding towards me on horseback. It was Easter Monday, and there appeared nothing surprising about their taking a ride outside the city on that day. But as they approached they dismounted and waited as though they expected to see me.

The coolies halted and I alighted from my chair, then Mr. Glastone Porteous gripped my hand and introduced himself, followed by Mr. Metcalf and Mr. Albert Allen. They told me there were others waiting farther along the road, and asked if I would care to ride one of their horses.

They assisted me into the saddle.

"How did you know?" I asked.

"The military in the capital received a telephone message this morning saying that you would be coming escorted by their soldiers," they told me.

At the top of a slight incline I saw the waiting men. To me it seemed a huge crowd, but Mr. Porteous explained that it would have been greater had the authorities not insisted on the women remaining within the safety of the city wall.

As we approached they burst into the doxology. My heart leaped for joy, lifting me out of my weariness, as I remembered his presence. I had come from the shadows but the light had accompanied me. A longing to give my freedom back to God possessed me.

I was asked to remain on the horse until they had taken a photograph. There followed much shaking of hands and exchanging of greetings. Mr. Ting and Mr. Yang, middlemen from Hunan, were there: their faces like friendly old clocks in a well-loved home.

Immediately my identity had been established Mr. Jack Graham, without getting off his horse, turned and galloped back to the city to telegraph Shanghai.

Someone gave me a clean handkerchief in exchange for the dirty blue rag which had served its purpose. Someone also offered lemonade, another chocolate.

The following day Dr. Yu came to examine me and the British Consul took me in his car to the private ward of the CMS hospital.

Within a week of my liberation dear Rose was by my bedside. A journey that would have taken months in the early days, and a fortnight by steamer and train at that time, was accomplished by air in a day and a half. It seemed a miracle.

Our joy was full, our cup running over .

13

AT THE STAMS' HOME

"THE YEAR AND A HALF OF SEPARATION seemed to belong to another world and it was as if we had never parted," Rose wrote. "No words can describe our joy and heartfelt praise to God as we met again. The Lord has done exceedingly above what we could ask or think. 'O magnify the Lord with me and let us exalt his name together'."

Rose had been in Shanghai during the latter months of my captivity. In Easter week they had been meditating on Acts chapter 12. As the leader read the story of Peter's release from prison, the phrase "Easter time" arrested her. She prayed repeatedly during the following days, "Lord, it's Easter time – do it again." Easter Day and the day following passed without news. On the Tuesday morning at breakfast with Mr. and Mrs. Griffin, who had been in the Training Home with me, a messenger arrived with two telegrams. Mr. Griffin* fetched a code book, but at a glance knew that one number meant "released". He had been looking for it in every telegram. He recognised also the code number of my name.

"Your husband's release," he told Rose.

*He had been with me in language school, and eventually became Home Director in North America.

She took a firm grip of herself.

"Better make sure it doesn't say 'not released'," she said, frightened of further disappointment.

"It's true, Rose dear, it's true," Mrs. Griffin gasped, when every word had been decoded. Their tears could not be withheld as they rushed to share the news with Mr. Gibb and others in the house and Mission Home.

That afternoon there was a thanksgiving service before Mr. Gibb sailed for England, praise and gratitude ascending to God.

Two days went by, then a further telegram from Yunnan suggested that, as I needed immediate and prolonged medical treatment, Rose should travel to be with me. By road and river it was a long journey, so friends advised she went by air. Inwardly she trembled. Flying in China was in its infancy. It was her first flight and the small aircraft ran into rough weather, but when she walked through the doors of the Church Missionary Society hospital, the duration of the journey reduced to a fraction, her heart was glad. She wrote at the end of May:

You will realise how timely the deliverance was when I tell you that the doctor's opinion is that my dear husband could not have survived longer than ten days had he not been set free. My husband is being kept in bed, rest being the only remedy to bring back the heart action to normal. It is his seventh week now and we do not know how much longer will be necessary, therefore we cannot make plans for the future . . . From skin and bones my husband has regained his normal weight again. He was suffering from pleurisy, bronchitis, beri-beri, and sprue, but the two former are now quite better.

Four weeks later the doctor gave his consent for me to

make a few rounds in my room daily, checking my pulse before and after. During these weeks Rose shared with me her experiences. The martyrdom of John and Betty Stam had been a terrible shock. Her newspaper gave a brief account of what took place and of how triumphantly they died, but she dare not read a second newspaper which spelt out the tragic details.

During that first Christmas much sympathy was shown to her as she entered into the festive season with the Hayman children, helping to fill their stockings with gifts, and preparing one as a surprise for Mrs. Hayman.

For several months the doctors would not allow me to go on furlough, and it was not until the late summer that we began our journey home, arriving in Marseilles on October 2. First we went to Rose's home. At La Côte-aux-Fées her mother, twelve brothers and sisters, with their husbands and wives, were waiting. The reception can be imagined. Our spirits lifted. There were tears and fountains of joy, and the world was beautiful again.

In England, my family had never been so happy. There was an avalanche of requests to tell of our experiences, but as I still had a long convalescence ahead, engagements were restricted. Our first public meeting was on November 6, at the Albert Hall, Manchester, chaired by the Rev. W. H. Aldis, the CIM Home Director. He said that many had asked why God had allowed my prolonged captivity. He suggested three possible purposes. First, so that there should be a witness to the Gospel in the Communist camps. Second, so that God's grace should be made manifest in the endurance and faithfulness of his children. Third, so that God's power should be made known in our deliverance.

Tribute was paid to Mr. Becker's untiring efforts to negotiate our release; to the Chinese messengers who risked their lives, not forgetting our cook Su En-lin who had voluntarily shared Grace Emblen's captivity, and even offered to take her place.

The CIM China Council at its one hundred and seventy-ninth session, in Shanghai, placed on record their gratitude to Mr. Becker. The minute was illuminated upon vellum and bound in volume-form for presentation to him.

To Mr. Hermann Becker who, with persistent hope in God, had for more than twelve months sought by every available means to give succour to our brethren, Messrs. Hayman and Bosshardt, and on behalf of the Hunan Provincial Authorities to negotiate terms for release, refusing to be turned from his purpose by disappointments or delays, but by his messengers following up the Communist forces from place to place and with resourceful skill leaving no means untried which might be blessed to the end in view.

Public meetings were held in London, Birmingham, Bournemouth, Southport, and throughout the country, large gatherings numbering up to 2,000 people.

My local paper reported a reception given for me by the Methodist Layman's Missionary Group.

Mr. Bosshardt has been resting at his sister's home in Chorlton for the last few months and looks almost a different man to the haggard and nerve-shattered figure who came to Manchester . . . Telling of the amazing zeal of the Chinese Reds in their own beliefs and hopes for a new world, he said their zeal was truly amazing. "They believe themselves to be part of the new world-wide revolution. The Red army, which numbered over 20,000, were mostly under 25, perhaps the majority under 20. They were just youths but full of vigour and zeal for their cause and I used to look at them and covet them for Christ. They were not ashamed to say that they were Reds and Communists and to speak of what they were doing. Every little village we passed through they left their mark and slogans behind."

Their headline was *Mr. Bosshardt plans to return to land of his captivity.* It was true, but the doctors held me back. In 1938 we addressed meetings in Switzerland, the number still restricted, although I was now fit enough to explore, revelling in the Alps and lovely pinewoods.

Then a cyclone struck the forest north of La Cote and felled a thousand trees in a few moments. The village was spared, though the château nearby was unroofed.

Driven home by the fearful threatening sky, we had entered the house just five minutes when the deluge came. It was awesome. A few more minutes and it was all over, but what a sight awaited our eyes. Prostrate giants, uprooted or snapped in two were flung in all directions. The storm had ploughed its way through the forest in an unbelievable manner.

Rose and I spoke at the International Bible Conference at Thun and at the Christian Convention at Morges, where sixteen nationalities were represented. We went on to the annual missionary meetings of the French-speaking Swiss Brethren, then returned to England for more gatherings, spending December on a tour arranged by the Scottish CIM Secretaries. We had Christmas with my parents in Manchester, returning to Switzerland at the end of January.

It was thrilling to speak in my father's home town, Winterthur, which he had left fifty-eight years before, and also to spend a short time in my mother's native village of Oberuzwil.

Sunday morning, June 11, found us with the worshippers at La Chappele. Chinese banners of red satin and gold, and colourful embroideries, hung up in preparation for a missionary demonstration in the evening, together with a floral display left over from a wedding the day before, lent a festive air. The service was in progress when, to our surprise, the presiding elder called out the names of Rose and myself and asked us to sit on the vacant front bench. With a twinkle in his eye, he informed the congregation that it was our wedding anniversary, and being the first in our home village, he thought it proper to bring us forward for a word of exhortation. He descended from the pulpit to give us the kiss of benediction and a gift book (in place of the family Bible usually given to the bridegroom after the ceremony).

After a few days in Belgium we returned to England to say our farewells in Manchester. The doctor had not given permission for our return to China, but we were going to America.

"Then you will be halfway to China," Mr. Aldis, the Home Director, told us.

We arrived in New York on October 17, 1939, with a schedule of speaking engagements. Because of the war in Europe we had left England with the lights blacked out. Our journey across the Atlantic, zig-zagging to avoid enemy attack, had been thoroughly miserable, but New York harbour twinkled with light. We stood in silence, holding each other close.

A priority was to visit John Stam's family in New Jersey. Mr. Stam had written after learning of the tragedy in China:

Our dear children, John and Betty, have gone to be

with the Lord. They loved him. They served him and now they are with him. What could be more glorious? It is true, the manner in which they were sent out of this world was a shock to us all, but whatever of suffering they might have endured is now past, and they are both infinitely blessed with the joys of heaven.

As for those of us who have been left behind, we are reminded by a telegram from one of John's former schoolmates, "Remember, you gave John to God, not to China." Our hearts, though bowed for a little while with sadness, answered, "Amen." We are sure that our dear brother and sister, Dr. and Mrs. C. E. Scott, both join us in saying, "The Lord gave, and the Lord hath taken away; blessed be the name of the Lord."

"Let us say the right words," we prayed as our train arrived in the city of Paterson, but words were not necessary. John's brother, Jacob, met us at the station, tall, cheery, a man of God. When we arrived at the Stams' home in the older part of the city, John's mother opened her large heart and welcomed us in. Peter Stam, John's father, was in hospital, but we were able to visit him and share our experiences. He was the founder of the Star Hope Mission, where we held our meetings, and was loved throughout the city for his ministry among the poor and elderly and to those in prison. During our captivity he had organised prayer on our behalf.

Our bedroom was where John Stam was born.

Why did they have to die? Why did God deliver Mr. Hayman and myself from the Communists and not John and Betty? But the question was not asked by the family. They spoke of the infinite wisdom and goodness of God, of his divine will; and of the seven hundred students who had stood up in the Memorial Service held in the Moody Bible

Institute, to consecrate their lives to missionary work wherever God might call them.

We left the Stams cherishing a new experience of God.

We were almost twelve months in America and Canada. Our first base was Philadelphia where we spent a few months. After visits in Canada around Toronto, we went on through Chicago, Wisconsin and on to Los Angeles which we used as a centre for some months. Then we travelled north to Vancouver, on the way speaking at Portland, Oregon, Salem, Tacoma, Bellingham and Yakima. Later we went to Calgary and Prairie Bible Institute, Three Hills, Alberta, where I met my brother, by adoption, whom I had not seen since he emigrated to Canada when he was nineteen and I was seven.

Our reunion took place in the Tabernacle. I had finished speaking when the chairman rose and said: "I think Mr. Bosshardt's brother is here. Will he please come forward?" Charlie had been present most of the time I was speaking. He came forward from the back of the hall and there was a dramatic moment as we shook hands in front of the great audience.

My father's eightieth birthday, September 16, 1940, found us aboard the *Empress of Russia,* with nearly fifty other missionaries, bound for Shanghi. We stopped briefly in Japan. In Shanghai we learned that Arnolis Hayman and his wife Rhoda had invited us to stay in their apartment over the Mission's business department. On our first Sunday there I went with Arnolis to the prison immediately after breakfast. We were delegated to the condemned prisoners' section. Each condemned man had a cubicle opening on to a wide concrete passage. Everything was scrupulously clean, but they had no privacy and no furnishing other than a garbage can and two blankets. Mr. Hayman started at one end and I at the other speaking to each man individually. For the most part, as they pressed against the bars, they were pleased to see us. Although condemned some had been waiting long for execution. One fellow had been converted during his two years there and spent his day reading the Bible. There were about thirty men in all.

A party of missionaries was leaving for the interior by a northern route to evade the Japanese who were occupying large parts of China, but we were not allowed to join them. The Kiangwan Bible Seminary needed a missionary couple temporarily to oversee their men's hostel, and we were invited to take up this opportunity. My reaction was that we would not wish to be involved in any work that would hinder our return to the interior, but when we had been assured it would only be for about two months we were much happier.

I continued visiting the prison in Shanghai. A lad of eighteen, found guilty of murder, never took his eyes off me when I spoke to him and I believe that he grasped that salvation is a gift from God. Another prisoner burst out: "The Saviour is only for those who have money: they can go to Heaven." I told him the parable of the rich man and Lazarus. When I returned the following week he was waiting for me, attentive, and hungry to know more.

On Christmas day we went to the Free Christian Church in Shanghai, where Bishop Houghton, our new General Director, was speaking. After the service Arnolis came across and shook hands with me. The same thought was in both our minds.

"Emmanuel," he said.

The angels sang, and Heaven rejoiced, but no more than on that Christmas day in captivity.

Our finest Christmas present was news that very day that we would be joining a party leaving for the interior in January.

It will be thrilling to see the mountains of Kweichow once again and to hear folks talk good Mandarin, and to mix with the country folks and be one with them as we cannot seem to be within this foreign place. We are to take in a lot of stores for the missionaries of the west who have been cut off from the coast for so long.

We travelled by boat, train and bus with Yunnan missionaries, all of us going via the Burma Road. The doctor had stipulated his conditions after examining me. First, I must not be far from a doctor; second, I must be in a place where there was nourishing food; third, I must not take on too much responsibility. Miss Köhler's station in Tungchow fulfilled the conditions, having an altitude that tempered the climate, a wonderful vegetable garden, with orchard and cows, and she having as much experience as, or more, than many doctors.

We sailed from Shanghai for Rangoon. There were troublesome formalities on entering Burma. Shanghai was expected to fall to the Japanese, and the Mission was preparing a war-time headquarters in Chungking.

In Rangoon we stayed at the Baptist Mission House, a centre hallowed by the residence of Judson. News of air raids on the Burma Road sent us to our knees that we might get safely through.

Having four truck loads of luggage we were delayed for a few weeks by the customs in Burma, but when we did get out we made good progress, the road on the Burma side being good. There were seven of us in the party and we divided ourselves into various truck cabs. We crossed a bridge, at the foot of a hill, and found ourselves once again in Free China.

"It's wonderful to be back," I said to Rose.

Her face was radiant.

Formalities took half a day, but the customs officials were well disposed to us. We crossed the Salween river, and descended from a tremendous height round hairpin bends before reaching Tali where there was a CIM compound. Here we refreshed ourselves, and washed off the dust. For two nights we had been unable to undress. We hurried on to Siakwan to see seven baptisms in the lake. Each of the candidates prayed publicly and I spoke.

On Good Friday, in Kunming, the first air raid warning sounded before we finished family prayers, which meant rushing out of the city gates to shelter in the fields. After three hours the all-clear went, but half-way through lunch we heard the drone of aircraft, and looking out saw twenty-seven, in perfect formation. They dropped their bombs and from the rising smoke we guessed our chapel had been hit. Our goods and stores were in it. We ran along the road, but turning a corner saw the chapel standing, a building opposite ablaze.

Instead of joining Miss Kohler's station, we were unexpectedly designated to take charge of the newly opened station of Panhsien, unattended by missionaries for a year. The four baptised Christians needed shepherding and teaching. The appointment hardly met the doctor's orders, and we were bitterly disappointed not to have at least a year with Miss Köhler.

A CIM missionary, Mr. Pike, who first prospected the opening of Panhsien twelve years before, had been captured and killed by bandits. In 1931 his daughter accompanied her mother to take her father's place, and later his son, Walter Pike, joined them. Alison Pike was to become Mrs. Rowland Butler, wife of a regional director.

We left Kunming by train on Monday morning on a newly opened track. When I saw my ticket I asked why we had been booked fourth class. It was the only class, which meant sitting on our luggage in bare trucks, but we remembered Hudson Taylor, who when asked why he always travelled third class, replied because there was no fourth.

We travelled to Kuching, and from there took a bus, but before entering Kweichow the steering broke and the bus went into a gully. We crawled out through a window, thankful to be alive.

Kweichow is a lovely province. The valleys are narrow between the mountains, but the hillside was covered with flowers, wild roses, and flowering shrubs, including azaleas. At a stopping place we met a member of the British Embassy who gave us a lift in his new car. He had come from Burma and was travelling to Chungking. Now progress was rapid. We quickly passed through Tsingchen, where we had our honeymoon, and he dropped us at the compound in Kweiyang, before continuing his journey to Chungking.

Our visit to Miss Köhler was by way of "consolation". We were to be four stages from Kweiyang, two of which could be travelled by car on the new motor road.

Miss Köhler had been in China since 1898, and eventually stayed in Kweichow for fifty years, with only one furlough. Between 1908 and 1951 she never left China. She was thirsty for news of friends and relatives in Switzerland. We found her in the Mission compound, treating patients, although it was evening. She was sixty-one at this time and working alone, her home one of the seven wonders of the province. She planned it and superintended the building and paid for it from her savings and special gifts. She bought a hillside and in levelling a place to build acquired much stone, so that most of her house and the other buildings were of stone, enclosed by a stone wall. Her house had fourteen rooms, besides a chapel and outhouses, a dispensary and bookroom. Her garden contained all kinds of flowers and fruit, much grown from seed sent by her brother. The Chinese called her grandmother and venerable teacher and whole families owed their lives to her skill. We visited the Christian cemetery with her.

"I have more of my people in Heaven than on earth," she said.

Some of the graves were of Christians who had met violent deaths. Her adopted son was murdered in daylight outside her house on market day because of his stand against evil. (Later his only son Koh Chi-En was executed by the Communists after months in prison. Not one of the first round of shots touched him as he sang praises to God. He fell when the order was given for the second round.)

In life we can sometimes accept the big trials more easily than the small disappointments. We had been able to take my captivity as being in the purposes of God. It was harder to accept that we could not remain with Miss Kôhler.

14

PANHSIEN

ROSE COULD NOT TRUST HERSELF TO SPEAK when the day came to say goodbye to Louie Köhler, who had treated us so royally. She had presented me with a pair of cloth shoes, specially made, and given velvet embroidered ones to Rose. She loaded us with what she could ill spare herself and sent a Chinese boy to accompany us.

We had felt cherished with her, but God was going before us, and when we arrived in Panhsien in June we found a house prepared, and a Chinese cook. Our neighbours in Anshun, seven stages away, were Mr. and Mrs. Leslie Lyall. On our first Sunday about fifty people crowded into the guest hall, leading from our courtyard, and a few stayed behind after the service for discussion. There was no chapel in Panhsien. None of our members or supporters were influential or rich, most were grimly poor, but God's work had never been dependent on the wealth of man.

It was good to be back in harness after our long absence from the country and people we loved, to know that soon we would be merged into the community, new faces becoming familiar and precious. We bought goats and found a goat-herd, a believer as yet illiterate, who also carried our water from the river and well, drinking water being some distance away. We lived at close quarters with our neighbours and kept open house, finding them curious about our possessions and all that we did.

There were four church members in the city, plus many adherents. Since the large evacuation of missionaries from China in 1927 there had been a conviction that the missionary's job was to develop an indigenous church. Ten years seemed a reasonable period starting from scratch to organise, develop, encourage, and then withdraw to repeat the cycle elsewhere. Panhsien looked an ideal base for testing this theory, although our four members would not have impressed a job consultant as the most promising group on which to build. Mrs. Koh Lai, who was seventy when she was converted, was blind and illiterate (she became a powerful Christian witness). Huan San Niang, our cook, was forty; she had persevered with her lessons and was able to follow the Bible reading in the service. Mr. Fu, about forty-five, could read more or less fluently having had two years' schooling. Our fourth member, Mr. Kao, somewhat more. These were the first that God called, and it took them a little while to discover their responsibilities and what God was asking of them. Having struggled for a year without a missionary, they favoured sitting back, letting us make all the suggestions, but we started a monthly church business meeting which soon began to develop their initiative. We wrote home:

How we would love you to drop in and see us. What a stirring welcome the Christians would give you. We are getting into running order. The devil is busy and several who attended our services are being persecuted by their families, sometimes the women being beaten by unbelieving husbands. One old woman from the country has been turned out of her home. Her son has stolen her fields and will not feed her. There are about twelve meetings a week including family prayers to which our neighbours come. Last week we used a flannelgraph for the first time. We saw this method used in America and were intrigued. I visited the chief magistrate and found him young and alert. He told us that he had read much of the Old and New Testaments, but was not a Christian. I asked permission to visit the prisons but he politely refused saying that he thought we had enough work preaching to those outside. Many soldiers are passing through Panhsien, but we do not know their destination. This sends the price of food soaring . . . While I am writing Rose has quite a crowd of women round her listening to the Gospel. We are selling a lot of Bibles and there are daily opportunities for witness.

Panhsien was growing on us. The city was beautifully situated between the mountains and was bigger than it had first appeared, with more development outside the city walls than in. Our own home, inside, was simply furnished, with a garden where we grew flowers and vegetables. Our dahlias gave great delight. There were sometimes visitors like Mr. and Mrs. Jensen from Denmark; Mr. Wang from Kweiyang; Mr. Cyril Weller (now OMF director in the Philippines) who came to continue his language studies, and Miss Hannah Chen, Rose's bridesmaid. Mr. Will Austin and his wife, co-workers for a time, had a fruitful ministry.

Our guest hall was so full on Sundays that at one business meeting a member stood up and urged that we should set aside a time to pray for one thing – a chapel of our own. The suggestion echoed in most hearts, so it was fixed that there should be thirty minutes' prayer each Sunday between the communion services and the preaching service. Although we had no material resources faith fairly blazed in those prayer gatherings.

Not many weeks later, on a Saturday evening, the answer came. A businessman, whose daughter was a Christian, came to almost demand that we took over the middle storey of his fine three-storeyed building, centrally situated, over his medicine shop, reached by an outer stairway. Soldiers had been using it as a billet when passing through Panhsien and our presence would keep them out. The rent was nominal, but we knew it had been fixed in heaven.

"Start your services there tomorrow," he urged.

When I said this would not be possible, he asked for permission immediately to fix our sign-board over the building declaring it was ours. We called the church members together and they gladly accepted praising God for this provision. Early on the Monday morning a group of us arrived to clean and furnish the new premises, but we had been there only a few minutes when we heard footsteps stamping up the staircase.

A group of soldiers burst in. It was a tense moment, as I quietly explained that this was our meeting place and asked them to find other quarters. As they clattered down the steps our hearts overflowed with thanksgiving.

The provision of this chapel, in answer to prayer, was talked about throughout the city.

At first it looked too big. Our backless seats looked lost, but by degrees we had new pews, first four, then eight, and so on, all paid for by local Christians. A member carved a beautiful communion table with a Chinese translation of Christ's words: "Do this in remembrance of me." The top was black lacquered, a speciality of the province, as clear as a mirror. The table was given as a memorial to the first pastor, Mr. Crapuchettes, who was killed in a road accident.

We decorated the chapel for our first Christmas, and after the service went down together, through the East

Gate, across the market place, to the river, a curious crowd following. Cyril Weller had his accordion and led the singing as one man and three women were immersed in baptism by me, there being no Chinese evangelist. We returned to the chapel for Chinese dainties, sun-flower seeds, puffed rice cakes in sugar water, and melon slices; we sang carols and in the evening had another service. The following Sunday we welcomed the newly baptised to the communion table.

Because the world was at war, our letters took up to nine months to reach home, and we heard from our families infrequently. Food, clothing and household commodities soared in price, but we lacked nothing.

In 1943 Rose received permission to visit the women's prison and I the men's. They were squalid and dirty, with sickness rife. Those who had no friends or relatives to bring them food were left to starve. For the better-off it was easier, some having private apartments. A few prisoners made straw sandals or waited on the wealthier for scraps of food. Conditions were so frightening that I begged the chief magistrate to give me the rice water which was normally thrown away. This provided nourishment and I arranged for two pails of it to be delivered daily.

When American soldiers passed through Panhsien their cooks bought glutinous rice, but burned it by cooking it like ordinary rice. They were throwing it away when I approached their officer and asked if I could have it for the prisoners. He would not believe what I told him, so he came along to see for himself. The men came with their bowls and pushed them through the bars for their portion, concerned it would run out before their turn. When I turned to him there were tears in his eyes.

"I wouldn't have believed it," he said.

The years went by, our ministry continuing quietly,

new workers joining us, itinerating in the district, a holiday in Anshun in the Lyalls' home, a conference for thirty-six missionaries in Kweiyang, settling in a new home with a Chinese enclosed garden at the rear, Grace Emblen visiting us for six weeks until her furlough, seven Red Cross girls staying the night, until Christmas Eve 1945 found us singing carols at the American army camp, and Rose convalescing from a serious illness. I wrote after a visit from Miss Köhler:

How glad I was to have Louie Köhler here. We really thought Rose was leaving us, but the Lord had mercy. The fever continued for five days and then, after sponging with alcohol, her temperature dropped suddenly below normal, after much sweating. For the next nine days she seemed to be making a good recovery and had just begun to get up and take her meals more or less normally when up went the temperature again. It was dangerously high, 105 degrees and over. She wanted to sleep and so we tried to get some, too, but soon we heard her groaning and these groans becoming fainter and her breathing, which had been laboured, seemed to stop. I called for Louie. Rose seemed to be slipping away, but prayer changes things. We were all gathered round the bed of my dear one. Mrs. T'an, the devoted Bible woman had come and a Chinese doctor and were just waiting. Suddenly Rose opened her eyes and said, "Is that you Mrs. T'an?" Then she looked and saw Miss Köhler and said: "Are you here Louie? Is there anything wrong?" Her temperature dropped to normal in about two hours. There were anxious times after that, but she pulled through.

While Rose was still walking with difficulty, and being

called to far too many maternity cases, we were joined for a period by Brian Bell, a young New Zealander, who had been in China three and a half years. His arrival was a tonic.

In Autumn, 1945 we had baptised Samuel T'ang, a very bright boy at the secondary school, whose father had been an evangelist in Yunnan. His father came to live in Panhsien before there was a church. He had lost his Christian witness, and became an opium addict. Yet he taught his three daughters and Samuel about Jesus. When our mission opened its work his wife brought Samuel along but the father never came.

At first Samuel showed little interest, being influenced by other youngsters, then his father died and he found himself, as the only male descendant, head of the home. Reading in bed by the light of a candle, his bed curtains caught fire, and he was badly burned trying to extinguish the flames. He came to us twice daily and Mrs. T'an not only renewed the bandages but told him more of Christ, with the result that he was converted and utterly transformed, making an open stand before his school mates. After his baptism his spiritual growth continued and we began to see him as a leader in the future years. Indeed, he felt God was calling him.

In 1946 I was chaplain to an American camp outside the city, conducting Sunday services, writing letters, and taking a funeral service now and again. For months up to twelve men came for supper until they built their mess.

That same year while on holiday in Kweiyang we were offered free transport to our old church at Tsunyi. It was my first visit since my captivity and we were overwhelmed with kindness. Mr. Lui, the deacon, who had stood with us in the famine, was the same genial warm friend as ever, and it was a great joy to see the progress that the church had maintained, although there had been no missionary recently.

On August 3, 1947, it was Maman Piaget's ninetieth birthday and we were granted our furlough a few months early to be at the celebration in Switzerland. We travelled across India, boarding a liner from Bombay to England, and after a quick visit to Manchester, made our way to Switzerland, arriving three days before her birthday. They said we would not make it, but God saw us through.

Maman's strength survived a day crowded with emotion, with comings and goings, speeches and singing, worshipping and feasting. Early in the morning the children came to sing for her and give their presents. At the morning service, it being a Sunday, I was asked to play the organ voluntary and selected "He shall feed his flock." Cousin Luc, in the absence of his father the chief elder, led the service. Members of the family took part and Maman's eldest grandchild, Georges-Ali Maire preached the sermon. Cousin Luc spoke at the communion service which followed. Each house had a full table of guests for dinner and afterwards we went to Maman's little wood outside the village, where there was a summer-house with easy chairs and palliases. Children were everywhere, four generations gathering together. There were ninety-six family members present and about thirty absent. There was hymn-singing in the wood, official and private photographs and a picnic tea. And there, in the midst, was Maman, serene, enjoying every minute, like a queen. Maman Piaget died just before her ninety-first birthday after falling and breaking her hip.

A few months after we returned to China in 1948, my father died and my mother who had been so strong and active began to show signs of weariness. She was eighty-six.

We wondered if we should stay longer with her, but subsequent events proved we were right not to delay our return to Panhsien, for time was short for missionaries in China.

The church helped Samuel T'ang to go to a Bible Seminary, where the principal was Marcus Cheng, a well-known respected Christian pastor. It was our intention that at the end of his three-year course Samuel would come back and after a period together we would hand over to him, if the church would call him as their pastor. Our intention then was to work in a neighbouring county town and be on hand for consultation or Bible teaching. But this was not to be.

Before Samuel was through his studies the Communists took over Chungking where he was studying. The seminary continued, but drastic changes were made. Foreign missionary teaching and money was banned. Marcus Cheng believed that Christians should be loyal citizens to whatever authority was in power if this could be done without compromising the Gospel. For a time it seemed he could do this.

During 1950 there was a field conference in Kweiyan. Although we were much refreshed, our minds were exercised by the advance of the Red army and the inability of the central government to halt it. Then our mission gave notice that any missionary was free to leave China if he wished. A special letter was sent to us, as we had already suffered at the hands of the Communists. After prayer, we believed that while the mission remained in China we should also stay.

Our city was fearful of what would happen under a Communist regime, so it was a surprise to find myself with the welcoming committee. This had not been pre-arranged! On the evening they were expected I was asked to loan my pressure lamp as the advancing troops were expected after dark. We had been three days without officials, anxious days, the government having withdrawn to Yunnan. I did not want to part with such a useful article. It needed careful coaxing so in the end I accompanied the lamp.

We went up the hill along the motor-road and waited. Lower down the road was lined with subdued scholars from the schools, and representatives of the people. When the soldiers arrived bows and salutes were exchanged.

Communist rule came to Panhsien without a shot.

As we formed a procession to enter the city the Communists burst out with a violent anti-Chiang Kai Shek song that caught in our throats.

The new authority placarded the city thanking the people for their welcome. Our Christmas programme in the church went ahead. The good behaviour of the troops, their willingness to share in menial tasks, their concern for the weak and elderly, and their payment for anything they broke, or borrowed, allayed most fears.

The first to suffer were the landlords.

Ours, who shared his compound with us, had to give a mountain of rice which rose up in the centre of our courtyard. Though he would be impoverished, he felt it was bearable. As for the church the Christians had been steeled for persecution and it seemed unbelievable that we could continue as formerly. Our little primary school was allowed to function and our open-air services drew large crowds, Red soldiers listening on the fringe. A visit from officials passed cordially, although they said that no changes must be made without permission, so we carried on exactly as before with larger attendances.

These conditions lasted several months.

The first restriction was an order not to propagate our faith outside the chapel. That was the end of open-airs and home visitation.

Then they closed our school.

The headmaster and the head of the Roman Catholic school were summoned to the Yamen, where an irate official claimed the schools were inefficient. The headmasters protested, offering to compete with any school in any subject, but the offer was brushed aside. Later, we saw God's overruling. If the schools had remained open eventually we would have been compelled to use Communist primers and Communist teachers.

The beggars in the city were rounded up, given new clothes and sent to spy. They reported on everyone. What they ate, what they said, and where they went. When they had served their purpose they were denounced as worthless non-producers.

Terror swept the city as accusations were encouraged, no one knowing whom he could trust. Many were imprisoned, suicides became daily occurrences, twelve girls in their late teens and early twenties killing themselves in two weeks. One was a daughter of the owner of our chapel, who had taught in our school and was about to be baptised.

There were spies in our services. A zealous blind member, Mrs. Lou, who had prayed about "these terrible times" was followed home. Two comrades ordered her not to pray like that again.

Christians were asked to recant. One of our leaders, Mrs. Li, was frightened when her adopted Red soldier son tore down the Gospel texts in her home. He brain-washed her, outlining the Communist programme against religion, and she recanted, the only one of our seventy members to do so.

When each had to register we wondered how they would stand. When the register of Christians was complete we learned that some two hundred people had registered with their families as Christians.

15

THE COMMUNIST REGIME

DURING OUR EIGHTEEN MONTHS under the Communists we conducted three baptismal services. The first two were relaxed. At the third there were eleven candidates. We had sought permission, as country Christians were participating, but when no reply came we proceeded with a unanimous vote in favour of the usual ceremony at the riverside.

On a sunny February day, a crowd followed us to the river. There were three Red soldiers on the far bank. After the eleven candidates had been immersed, an elder explained the significance of baptism. At this point the Red soldiers signalled their displeasure, jumped on their cycles, and rushed for the bridge, meeting us as we were dispersing. The two Chinese who had taken part, the baptising elder, and the preacher, were arrested. When I protested, I was kicked and also led away for questioning.

In a room of soldiers, all dressed identically, I was unable to distinguish who were officers, as one and then another questioned me. Suddenly, a man who had been reclining on a bed sat up and snapped that I must be taken to a higher authority.

With a pistol in my back I was escorted by a soldier through the city streets.

Now officials probed my background, recording all I

said. When they came to the baptismal service I was asked if it was wise to immerse candidates on a winter's day. I said seventy had been baptised since our arrival in the city without harm.

After a homily, I was dismissed and allowed to go home. On leaving the Yamen I met Rose coming with extra garments and food. It was getting late and she had feared I would be detained, although throughout the city believers were praying. The other Christians had also been released but thanksgiving was mingled with uncertainty about the future.

After the second Christmas under Communist control we, together with the Catholic priest, were summoned to the chief magistrate and told to bring our passports. The old courtesy had gone: we were now unwanted, intruders, a burden to society. Our papers were retained and instructions given that we must not leave the town. We were prisoners within the city limits.

With us at this time were Mr. and Mrs. Alban Douglas,* a young couple from Canada. Alban had been in the city with us before his marriage. His wife who was expecting her first baby was taken ill with eclampsia during the Sunday morning service. We sat up with her all night. She had over twenty convulsions before, during and after the arrival of the baby, and for two weeks knew no one. The child was still-born. It had earlier been planned for Anna to go to the Mission hospital at Anshun but the authorities withheld a pass until it was unsafe to travel and the nurse we telephoned was refused a travel permit. It was all in the hands of Rose but God gave her the strength and with his help Anna came through.

*Alban is now a recognised Bible-teacher, and with Anna, a wonderful helpmate, is connected with the Prairie Bible Institute, Alberta.

Early in January, 1951, we had a letter from our headquarters that gave us a jolt. It told us to apply immediately for permission to leave China. The Mission had concluded that the presence of missionaries in China was an embarrassment to local Christians. We disagreed. But the letter advised us not to look at the local situation, which varied from province to province. When we told the Chinese Christians they wistfully urged us to stay. We sensed that if the British and Americans had to leave that as Swiss citizens our position might be better. Soon we came to the conclusion that the Mission knew better than we did, and had no doubt sought the mind of God, so we applied for permission to go, little thinking it would take five months, during which the Communists had our Swiss passports in their hands.

Our people, in common with everyone, were under instruction, attending Communist indoctrination classes several hours a week. A month after hearing of the advice from headquarters, the local people had learned more of the official attitude to foreigners and missionaries, and they told us: "Yes, it's right for you to go. Better for you, better for us."

The Catholic priest, a Belgian of deep spirituality, told us he would stay whatever the consequences. He was not yet thirty and utterly dedicated.*

During these months of waiting Samuel returned from the Bible seminary at Chungking, absolutely loyal to Christ and prepared to suffer. We had four wonderful weeks together. He took the attitude of the seminary which was to work with the Communists whenever possible. At a church

---

*A few months after our departure he was accused, put on trial for two weeks, then sentenced to banishment and escorted to Hong Kong.

business meeting he was elected pastor. He told the members that if he and his family could be supported (there were three children) he would give himself full-time to the church, but if not he would find a part-time job. He asked that a free-will offertory box be placed at the door for his support, not wanting to know who was contributing or how much.

He spoke, on his appointment, of the possibility of public meetings being banned and of the probability of secret meetings in homes. However, the first thing was to comply with the regulation to register the church. Most members had registered as individual Christians, giving them freedom to worship, but the registration of the church proved more difficult. Its history had to be written, foreign support of any type severed, and church accounts scrutinized. Samuel was mystified at the attitude of the authorities who sometimes flattered, sometimes advised, and sometimes threatened. They tried to make him incriminate himself, but he managed to avoid this, no doubt guided by the Holy Spirit.

Our little clinic was heavily taxed. Executions became commonplace. The proprietor of our house who had sought scrupulously to meet all demands was severely impoverished, yet continued to be urged to give "voluntarily" to various projects, and was severely condemned when he could not respond. A tenant drew up a petition claiming the proprietor had been a just man. While neighbours were signing the tenant was put in prison for a day, and told he must cease support for a landlord. The authorities arranged an accusation meeting for the proprietor. At first no one would give evidence, then words were thrust into their mouths. Doesn't he dress better than you? Eat better? Hasn't he oppressed you? But his tenants recalled his fair dealing during famine years, at harvest time, and the three days of feasting when his daughter married, and how they were given lodging in his home when they visited the city.

Failing to get sufficient evidence to sentence him to death the police arrived at the compound, where we also lived, after midnight, scaled the rear wall, and ordered us back to bed when we investigated. They called our cook, however, to get through our house to the front courtyard which gave access to the landlord's house.

A friend was instructed to knock gently at the door and ask for entrance. When it was opened the police rushed in. It was all rather strange as he was accessible at home or on the street during the day. The accusation was of falsifying property papers. He denied this but was arrested, never to return. His possessions were confiscated. When the authorities had taken their choice they called in the rabble from the street who left not a bowl or a pair of chopsticks. His wife came to see us utterly downcast. In daylight no one could show sympathy, only after dark and secretly. It was difficult to comfort her. Before this happened Mr. Fu often came to sit with me. He had a Bible which he read, but while his married daughter was a baptised believer, he was a Confucianist. "Until these men took over I thought the devil was a fabrication," he confided.

Mrs. Liu was a member of our church. Her husband bought stocks of standard medicine to open a "medicine shop", but took ill and died before the shop was opened. Mrs. Liu had the store of medicines in the house when the Communists came. She taught in our school but when this was closed she was without a job. To provide for herself, her mother and little boy, she set up a stall to sell some of her husband's clothing, and while she tended the stall she knitted socks and scarves to order. The authorities told her that if she were a business woman she could not also be an artisan: she must choose to earn her living by being in business or working with her hands. Later, during a search of every house in the town, she declared the medicine. Later accusation was made by someone, unknown of course, that either she or her husband had stolen it. They gave her time to think about it, and she came to see me in great distress, asking what to do. "Was it stolen"? I asked.

"No, no," she affirmed. "You know my husband would never do that."

"Then stick to the truth," I said. "Don't lie."

We prayed. Eight times they came demanding a confession. Finally, they sent two women professing to be her friends, who asked what would it matter to a dead man if she said he had stolen the goods. They urged her to consider the alternative.

"You'll be hounded to prison. What will happen to your eighty-year-old mother and your eight-year-old son?"

They left angrily, saying that she need not blame them when she languished in prison. They had done their best. Not long afterwards an officer arrived at her house. He brandished a pistol in her face.

"What's all this nonsense? Here's a declaration of your husband's guilt. Sign it."

"He did not steal. I will not lie."

"Sign it."

It was a command. What should she do? With a fast-beating heart she sent a cry to God. "What shall I do? Help me."

Quietly she said, "You say that my husband stole this medicine. Please tell me when?"

The officer gave the date.

"That's two and a half years ago," she said.

He nodded.

"My husband died three and a half years ago," she told

him, "and I'll take you to his grave where the date is carved in stone."

Without a word he placed the pistol in his hip pocket and left her home. Mrs. Liu came to me with a radiant face, to recount it all, and to praise the God who answers prayer and strengthens his servants.

A few months later her old mother yearned to be taken to her native place to die, to the loving German sisters who had nurtured her in the faith. The old lady could not walk and it was forbidden to ride in a sedan chair without written permission. When application was made, the request was not only granted, but coolies provided. They had, of course, to be paid for and this was done by selling the medicines which would have been confiscated if Mrs. Liu had not told the truth.

Anna Douglas, now convalescing, was eager to get away after her illness, yet month after month went by without word from the authorities. We thought we would set up a stall in the market to dispose of our surplus possessions, giving a percentage to refugees on everything sold, but this was nipped in the bud. An officer visited us. He told us we must not sell them, give them away or leave them behind. We were in a dilemma. The officer told us they wanted Alban's cycle, in good order, also our beautiful police dog.

Samuel advised us: "There's only one thing for you to do. Give to the authorities whatever you do not take."

Our letter to this effect was well received, the magistrate unable to conceal his delight at what they were going to receive. The letter finished by mentioning that we had been waiting several months for our pass. When he reached this paragraph his attitude changed. He threw the letter on the ground.

"What's this? Are you trying to buy your pass?" he raved.

He told me to rewrite the letter and if we really wished them to accept our property to make it clear by putting in the phrase "with a willing heart." This was done and our wait continued, then news came that the missionaries in Tsunyi had received permission to leave China. Not long afterwards I was notified to be at the Yamane at 7.30 the following morning. I was there on time, but the officer was not yet awake. I was treated politely and given tea while I waited. Eventually, he appeared with tousled hair, looking very sleepy. He talked to me while he washed.

"You wish to return home, to leave us," he said.

I mentioned our application for a pass five months earlier.

"When would you like to go?" he asked. "I will give you a letter to the magistrate in Kweiyang. If you take that you will get your passes."

It seemed too easy, so I was a bit apprehensive.

"Don't we need to advertise our going?" All other missionaries had to do this three times in the newspaper.

"No," he said, "all you want is a letter from me."

"Do we not need guarantors?"

"No," he said. "I will explain. We had a meeting to discuss you. Everyone said you were good people and so we are all your guarantors."

How wonderfully God had undertaken. If we had advertised, experience suggested that someone would have declared that I had broken the conditions of release by continuing to preach the Gospel.

The chief magistrate paid us a friendly visit. When he had left he sent a friend.

"If you really want to leave I advise you to leave your pressure cooker, your meat grinder. . . The magistrate is coming again and when he sees these things put aside, you will have your pass. This must be kept secret."

The magistrate returned bringing the precious letter. When I asked him if he would inspect what we were taking he lifted the lid of a box and said: "These are your personal effects, you will have absolutely no trouble."

The next morning the truck came to our door at 7 a.m. An hour earlier six men, who were prisoners, came to move our furniture. They left enough crockery for breakfast, the cook being responsible for handing this over later. What we left behind was listed five times in Chinese.

At last we were on our way.

At the checking-out station the driver said there was to be an examination of our goods. We waited until 1 p.m. then the police came and unloaded everything into the street, a huge crowd gathering to see this indignity to the foreigners. When everything had been examined in detail it had to be repacked. Then it started raining. At 4 p.m. we got away.

We were subject to eight such inspections, during our journey to Hong Kong, but what did it matter? We were met at the railway station in Hong Kong by members of CIM, including Bishop Houghton.

"Praise the Lord," he said. "You are here safe and sound. We've been so anxious for you. Now we can breathe again."

16

FRESH OPPORTUNITIES

EXPELLED FROM CHINA UPON WHICH OUR LIFE had been focused, like hundreds of other missionaries, we looked to God for our new assignment. It was easier for our bodies to leave than our hearts, but "When they persecute you in one city, flee to the next," became the word of the Lord to us. Among adjacent countries we thought of Laos, immediately south of Panhsien. There was no witness among the Chinese there and, with CIM's permission, the Swiss Brethren there invited us to join them.

For fifteen years I was to labour there, living in Pakse, but it was hard to visualise with serenity and detachment starting from scratch again, in the first place not knowing what language the Chinese spoke and whether it would mean learning a dialect.

To tell of our experiences in Laos would make another book, but, in brief, we found that the young people spoke Mandarin well, learning it at school. We started with the children and soon had a Sunday afternoon service for them. At first it prospered, then one Sunday not a child turned up. They had been forbidden to come by parents and teachers who believed we were spies sent by the French to report on what the Chinese were saying and doing. The suspicion had to be lived down.

Our first encouragement was when a Christian business-man from Phnom-penh, Cambodia, came to Pakse, and heard a lad singing, "Jesus loves me this I know." "Where did you learn that?" he asked, and so Mr. Loh was intro-duced to us. In our early years he came to Pakse fairly fre-quently to do business and usually stayed one month giving us much of his time.

We plunged into visiting, inviting our contacts to call on us, or we set a date for a meeting, but while some came and investigated from the other side of the street, when they saw an empty hall, none ventured in. Then a delega-tion of youths came, and asked if we would teach them French and English. Confidence was growing. We started daily classes. After each session we read the Bible, then sang and prayed. It was the start of a congregation.

Early in our stay in Laos, we received a letter from the Rev. David Yen, offering to assist us during the holidays. David Yen was a direct descendant of the favourite disci-ple of Confucius, seventy-six generations back. As such he was honoured as a child and carried to the sacred Con-fucian temple in a ceremonial chair as part of the feast day processions. When he was converted, he heard God's call to preach the Gospel to the poor. He entered the Bethel Bible School and later came to Kweichow, as it was among the poorest of China's provinces. We met him in Panhsien and later in Hong Kong when we had to leave China.

He arrived on Christmas Day for a month. He was thrilled to see the congregation for the evening programme and was under the impression that the students were Christians as by now they knew the hymns and could find their way in the Bible, but I explained that not one of them had so far been baptised or made an open confession. He believed they were but a step away, but during the special meetings there was no movement. He had been used in revival work and it distressed him to leave without baptisms. He did so, declaring that Laos was the hardest territory he had struck in all his travels in China, Hong Kong, the Philippines and Thailand, but his ministry was re-remembered and bore fruit in later years.

Today, David Yen is head of the Christian Faith Mission in Hong Kong, which he founded, with five thousand children in his various roof-top schools, orphanage, and secondary schools for under-privileged boys and girls.

After three years Rose and I went on furlough, arriving back in Pakse for our silver wedding anniversary in 1956. On our wedding day the Kweiyang church had given us four red satin banners with four Scripture passages written on them in gold. They were a little shabby, but still presentable, and on the anniversary we had them hung in the chapel. I wrote:

> The twenty missionaries who were with us a quarter of a century ago are now scattered throughout the world and a few are with the Lord. What a different China we find today! If a prophet had arisen then to tell us what the years would bring, how fantastic it would have all seemed. That China's doors should be closed against us, that we should be working in Laos – the future was all veiled for us and it still is, but we do take courage as we face another term, for "God is with us".

Although the Chinese were genuinely pleased to see us back in Laos, there was no rush to hear the Gospel. It was still hard going. Some of those we had relied on as a nucleus for a church had left Pakse, some studying in Saigon and some residing there. Mrs. Wang, a baptised Christian, was teaching in Donghen very far away. A few old students had returned to China for further education. But soon we had nine daily classes of English, which brought us near to the students, most of whom now had Bibles.

Since our expulsion from China our Mission had been renamed the Overseas Missionary Fellowship. Its Chinese magazine *Teng ta* (*Lighthouse*), published by the Christian Witness Press in Hong Kong, to attract the twenty million Chinese outside China, exceeded our expectations, comparing most favourably with other Chinese illustrated periodicals. We canvassed the town for subscriptions, making new contacts. Over a hundred subscribed.

In 1957 a survey team arrived in Laos. Our Mission was to investigate unevangelised areas. They trekked from village to village, from tribe to tribe. I wanted to detain them in Pakse for the Sunday service, but their faces were so set on proceeding without delay, that I did not care to broach the subject. After the survey Laos officially became an OMF field.

Highlights were Christmas and New Year, with record numbers gathering at Christmas services, for Bible readings, and to see pictures of the birth and life of Christ. There was a Christmas tree, lit with candles, later used by the Laos Christians, and at the leprosarium fifteen miles away.

One of our most thoughtful students was Henry. His composition written for his homework speaks for itself.

I live in a town of Laos; it is called Pakse, but I was not born there. I was born in Cholon, Vietnam. When I was young my family moved to Pakse, and now I am seventeen years old and I can speak Laotian, because I have lived here so long. There is a river that goes through Pakse. It comes from China and its name is Mekong. My home is near the bridge, so I and others always take a bath in the river. Pakse is not a great city, but a small town. There are about 20,000 people including Laotians, Chinese, French, Swiss, Indians, Americans, Vietnamese, and the Chinese are the most important of all. . . We learn English here every day with a Swiss pastor in the church. He teaches us English using *Kaiming Second English Book* and the Holy Bible, so that we know that Jesus saves us from sin. This morning about 9 o'clock I was going to our teacher's home to see him. Usually we go to study at 7.15 a.m., but today I did not go to study because he is ill. He caught a cold. I hope he is now better. When I went upstairs he was glad to see me I think! Mrs. Bosshardt was not at home so he was all alone. I talked with him a good deal, sometimes about the Bible and sometimes about his country – Switzerland.

One day Henry asked for baptism. At first he had put up with the Bible reading and was not much influenced. But then he began to take notice. We were at breakfast prior to the baptismal services when his sister appeared and asked if Henry was to be baptised. When we replied in the affirmative she said, "No. Our parents forbid it."

Mr. Loh, who spoke the same dialect as the parents, went to confer. They were angry and Henry was forbidden to come near us. His Bible and other literature was confiscated or burned, but he remained true and after a while the parents relented and he was allowed to attend first the language classes and then the services. He waited until he was almost twenty, believing he should obey his parents, then asked for baptism believing he had reached an age when he should obey God rather than man. He was baptised in the river, his companions watching, but his parents made it impossible for him to attend the communion service that night to be received into membership.

His conversion really marked the beginning of the church in Pakse.

The daily children's meetings were attended by up to fifty children, and the Sunday services grew to thirty.

There were more baptisms. The Bible class on Wednesday evenings fluctuated, but there were generally up to a dozen. Mr. Kuhn was now the OMF superintendent in Laos, and a full chapel of forty young men gathered to hear him on his first visit. What a treat for us to sit and listen! The church had been enlarged to take in the porch that ran along the front, previously used for cycles.

In 1963 we went on our last furlough, and during this Rose underwent a major operation at the Mildmay hospital, London, but made such a quick recovery that the doctor, who had prayed before he operated, told her, "God has healed you. You can go back to Laos."

In fact, we had reached the retiring age of sixty-five, but we made our application and the reply came from Mr. Oswald Sanders, our general director, that the Mission not only gave permission, but desired it, for there was no one to replace us.

About two years after our return Rose had a slight stroke which handicapped her, but she gradually recovered, learning to write and teach all over again. Then she had to go to Saigon with a liver complaint. After treatment in one of the finest hospitals she returned to Pakse, very much better.

For over two months she stayed with our dear friends Bernard and Helene Felix on the Plateau at Thateng, regaining her strength in the cooler atmosphere. They brought her down towards the end of April and she was her old self those first few days, then the extreme heat and humidity began to tell on her. The doctor ruled that she could not remain much longer in the tropics. Our time was not complete but his warnings could not be ignored.

She made an effort to pay a last visit to the leprosarium, partly to see how she stood up to the journey. On the way, climbing a hill to visit a former faithful servant, now married and crippled with a TB hip, the exertion proved too much and on returning to the car she was sick. On Saturday evening, Teacher Liu gave us a wonderful Chinese feast. It was brought to the house and Rose lay on the camp bed while ten guests sat around the table. She enjoyed everything so thoroughly, though, of course, she could only partake of very little of the dainties. On retiring at 9 p.m. she became violently ill.

The next morning her condition caused real alarm and we hurried for the doctor who assured us all would be well if she was kept quiet. He promised to come in the afternoon, but was delayed through an operation at the hospital and when he did appear, he hurried away again to fetch oxygen. But it was too late. At 8 p.m. Rose quietly stopped breathing and her spirit went to be with the Lord, whom she so ardently loved and so faithfully served.

Henry went to tell the other Christians. When they entered, they dropped to their knees and prayed a chain prayer, thanking God for the life lived among them, now returned to the heavenly home.

The car ordered for the next morning to take us to the railhead for Bangkok – the first step home – was cancelled.

The Chinese Christians were marvellous. When they knew I wished Rose to be among the Chinese in death as in life, they went out to the new cemetery, six kilometres away, to select a place and make arrangements. The service was advertised for 8 a.m. Long before that people arrived. Chairs and benches from the chapel had been brought over and others borrowed from neighbours, and when our three rooms, which opened out off each other, were crowded, they overflowed to the verandah and garden. Twelve nationalities were represented.

I spoke of my dear companion's thirty years in China and her fourteen in Laos, and her passport furnished me with an illustration. "This is my wife's passport," I said. "It was all in order, stamped officially, so that she could pass through Thailand and Italy to Switzerland. There would be no question about her entry there. Now she has gone to another country, a heavenly one, but her papers for that land were prepared when her name was written in the *Book of Life*. Is your passport for heaven in order?" I asked.

Our journey to the cemetery was a triumphant procession, singing through the mile-long street.

I wrote home:

Normally, we would have been boarding the boat for Europe this day, but the Lord had other plans for us. Rose was very weary and had her doubts of ever arriving to see her loved ones again. . . The only reason for our planning to return was the health of dear Rose. Thus I have no reason for leaving Laos at this time. We had prayed so much for someone to continue the work, but labourers are few. Now the Lord is recommissioning me to carry on for a little time.

On Thursday morning, Calvin [one of several students who were baptised] came with an exercise book containing a subscription list and an account of all expenses for the funeral and then handed me a considerable amount of money. All expenses had been met by the Chinese friends and the money was for me. I said I would pray as to how to use it, but someone remarked it was for me to get a holiday.

A memorial stone was laid on the grave on May 1 the following year. St. John chapter three, verse sixteen, in Chinese and French was carved on it, an empty cross surmounting it telling of the risen Lord. Shortly, I would return home.

It will not be easy to take leave of these dear friends, for I have been fifteen years and known many of them as children. So far there is no one in sight to shepherd the Christians and to continue the work. . . How glad one is to leave it all in the Lord's hand, he who is all wise and who is love. The weather has been exceeding hot and trying this year, partly because the rains came a month too early and steamed things up. When I remember how my dear one suffered from the heat last year, I rejoice that she is where "the sun shall never beat upon them, nor any scorching heat."

On the way to Europe, with other missionaries, I spent two days in the Holy Land. My sister Ida joined me for a month at La Côte-aux-Fées where I was in the bosom of the Piaget family. In October I was back in England believing I had said goodbye to the Chinese, now closer and dearer to my heart than even my own countrymen.

I was wrong.

During my absence hundreds of Chinese had arrived in Manchester. They had come to England as students, nurses, restaurant proprietors and staff, and right on my doorstep was the Chinese Christian Fellowship. In two books *The Chinese Church That Will Not Die* and *Stephen the Chinese Pastor* Mary Wang, Director of the Chinese Overseas Mission, had told of this ministry around the world.

I was desperately tired. Because of liver trouble I was on a strict diet. I was inclined to feel like a fish out of water but the Chinese Christian Fellowship was a wonderful comfort and help. I could do little more than attend their meetings and speak occasionally, and then I was asked to be an adviser on their committee. My contribution was modest because of such excellent Chinese leadership, but what joy to see their vigorous witness. They are *my* people.

Union Hall, from which I went to China as a young man, had never ceased to pray and support Rose and myself, along with other missionaries, and the pastor and members affectionately welcomed me back. The zeal, the dedication, the faith I had known as a youth were still there.

I have been thinking again of John and Betty Stam, who died for their faith on a Chinese hillside, while our lives were spared. Naturally, some talked of wasted lives. Forty years later we know how wrong they were. Although we gave ourselves in long years of Christian service, and saw a harvest, our influence was tiny in comparison. It was said that the tragedy opened the deep springs of faith and love in countless hearts. They still flow today. As their story is retold the vision continues to dawn on young people of the privilege of sacrifice and suffering in fellowship with Christ. We were called to live for Christ, they to die for him.

As I write *The Times*, London, has a China Trade Supplement telling how China, which has remained virtually closed to Westerners for more than twenty years is slowly opening its frontiers. It says: "Anyone applying for a tourist visa may be in luck, and businessmen offering the sort of trade for which the Chinese are looking should not find any difficulty."

What about missionaries? They have a role, but the future may be with young Chinese Christians, scattered over the face of the globe, who one day may join the tourists and businessmen to carry out Christ's great commission to their own people. Stephen Wang, founder of the Chinese Overseas Christian Mission said: "If China is to be evangelised it must be by the Chinese." They will surely know, as I have known, God's guiding hand.

> Can I doubt his tender mercies
> Who through life has been my guide.